Global Civics

Global Civics

Responsibilities and Rights in an Interdependent World

HAKAN ALTINAY

editor

BROOKINGS INSTITUTION PRESS
Washington, D.C.

Copyright © 2011
THE BROOKINGS INSTITUTION
1775 Massachusetts Avenue, N.W., Washington, DC 20036.
www.brookings.edu

All rights reserved. No part of this publication may be reproduced or
transmitted in any form or by any means without permission in writing
from the Brookings Institution Press.

Library of Congress Cataloging-in-Publication data is available.
ISBN 978-0-8157-2141-3 (pbk. : alk. paper)

9 8 7 6 5 4 3 2 1

Printed on acid-free paper

Typeset in Sabon and Ocean Sans

Composition by Cynthia Stock
Silver Spring, Maryland

Printed by R. R. Donnelley
Harrisonburg, Virginia

Contents

Foreword

The world as a ball of twine. Consider the interconnectedness that image implies, and one understands why more and more opinion makers, economists, politicians, and academics have increasingly emphasized the need for global cooperation as the world's nations and their citizens have become far more interdependent. In September 2008 the collapse of one investment bank in New York triggered a worldwide financial panic and the most serious economic slowdown experienced by the world in decades. In many domains such as financial stability, trade, control of nuclear or chemical weapons, protection against infectious disease, or the challenge of climate change, what happens in one country has major spillover effects on many other countries and often on the whole of humanity. Not everything is global, of course, and one should not forget the power and relevance of the very local; but many key challenges are indeed global and can only be managed with very strong cooperation among countries and regions.

A key economic idea, and one that harks all the way back to Hume's 1739 "Treatise on Human Nature," has been the concept of global public goods, derived from the older concept of national public goods. A pure public good is one that when consumed by some, does not diminish what others can consume and that once available, is available to all, without exclusion. In technical jargon, public goods are nonrivalrous and nonexcludable. Clean air is a classic example, as are national security (in a single-country context) and pure knowledge. A global public good that has received much recent attention, because of global warming, is the temperature of the atmosphere. Global financial stability and a well-functioning global trading system are other examples of global public goods.

The concept of global public goods allows global policy challenges to be analyzed in a rigorous way and allows policymakers to understand and explain the benefits of cooperation. Take my earlier example of global warming. Why should American or European taxpayers subsidize the building of clean or cleaner energy generation plants in India? The response is, on the face of it, simple: because the greenhouse gas emissions from Indian power plants have as much effect, per ton of carbon emitted, as greenhouse gases emitted in Chicago or Berlin. So by helping reduce carbon emissions in India, Americans and Europeans help to stabilize the temperature of the atmosphere, just as they would by mitigating emissions at home. But the same is true for Indians: by helping to finance emission reductions in Chicago or Berlin, they would also be helping themselves. This illustrates the nature of a global public good. But because India is much poorer than the United States or Germany, it is less able than those two Western nations to subsidize mitigation within its borders, let alone beyond them. And this, in turn, illustrates that at the heart of the problem of providing public goods lies the issue of distributing the burdens and benefits: who should shoulder what part of the burden of providing them?

This challenge exists both at the national and global levels. At the national level, governments, parliaments, and elections determine the distribution of benefits and costs. Sometimes the national debates become extremely heated and the politics very tough. But in the end, solutions are found and compromises are accepted; that is how nations function. There are institutions that mediate, facilitate the reaching of compromises, and ensure the implementation of the solutions agreed upon. There are legal sanctions for noncompliance.

It is clear that at the international level, these institutions either do not exist or are still very weak. The United Nations is not an international parliament. The United Nations Framework Convention on Climate Change can convene meetings on climate, but it has been extremely difficult to reach even a basic agreement. Despite its name, the International Monetary Fund is not a global central bank. The World Trade Organization is probably the institution with the greatest amount of global enforcement capacity, and even that is very limited. Given the continuing sovereignty of nation-states, the difference between national and international institutions is natural and understandable. And yet much of what needs to happen for cooperation to become more effective and to be able to "deliver" global public goods relates to the strengthening and development of these international institutions.

Comparing the global to the national level, there is an underlying, crucial ingredient of success that is different in the two settings. Citizens cooperate in a national community, pay their taxes, and are willing to participate in national defense because they have an emotional bond with each other, because they feel allegiance to the community and its symbols. It is the flag and the law, together, that make cooperation work. The flag alone would surely be insufficient, but the law alone also would not ensure a well-functioning community. If all behavior were to be governed strictly and only by individual self-interest and a cold-blooded calculation of benefits and costs, national communities would be very costly, if not impossible, to govern. A sense of "civics" is part of the cement that holds a community together, that reduces the "cost" of governing and enables the compromises that deliver the public goods.

This thoughtful book—partly written, partly assembled by Hakan Altinay—debates civics in a global context. The message from Altinay and from many of the distinguished contributors is that we cannot progress rapidly enough toward the global cooperation needed for the twenty-first century without the development of some form of "global civics." As someone who has taught courses on the economic calculus of global public goods and has tried to help produce them while holding office in international organizations, I wholeheartedly agree. It remains crucial to compute the costs and benefits of alternative scenarios and policies, and it remains necessary for citizens and nations to understand what they gain and what they pay to get that gain. Economists must and will be busy clarifying the options and their net costs and benefits. Self-interest will remain fundamental to the conduct of national policies. It should not, nor can it be, however, the only mechanism at work. For international cooperation to succeed in our increasingly interdependent world, our consciousness of being members of a global community has to strengthen, our perception of connectedness and solidarity has to deepen, and, at times, the willing sharing implicit in any community has to extend beyond national flags and borders. This book explores whether and how that will happen.

Kemal Derviş
Vice President, Global Economy and Development
Brookings Institution

Preface

This book is a culmination of many conversations that took place throughout 2009 and 2010. The basic framework for a global civics was first presented at a Brookings seminar in January 2009 and developed during a 2009 Yale World Fellowship. The first chapter here is based on two Brookings working papers, "The Case for Global Civics" and "Does Fairness Matter?" as well as the reactions to these papers we received from around the world.

It seemed imperative to present a wide range of views of what global civics means, so part one addresses global perspectives. A number of these views are presented as interviews, which I did between June and November 2010, with esteemed colleagues from around the world. The interviewees include Balveer Arora, former rector of Jawaharlal Nehru University in Delhi, and Jonathan Fanton, who has been the president of the New School for Social Research in New York, my own alma mater, and of the MacArthur Foundation in Chicago. Fanton has also served as the chairman of Human Rights Watch. I was also fortunate to have four outstanding academics, David Held, Thomas Pogge, Dani Rodrik, and Dingli Shen from four vital disciplines—political science, philosophy, economics, and international relations—and four august institutions—the London School of Economics, Yale, Harvard, and Fudan—involved in the interviews presented here. Two cherished colleagues, Andrey

Kortunov and Ivan Krastev, were kind enough to join this conversation. Kortunov is the president of the New Eurasia Foundation in Moscow, and Krastev is the chairman of the Center for Liberal Strategies in Sofia. More important, they are both exceptional in rendering their parts of the world intelligible for the rest of us, while being thoughtful participants themselves in numerous global conversations. Two more participants of international stature are Ricardo Lagos and Javier Solana. Lagos was the president of Chile between 2000 and 2006, and later served as the president of the Club of Madrid. Solana has served as the minister of foreign affairs in Spain, secretary general of NATO, and high representative for common foreign and security policy of the European Union. Very few people enjoy the near-universal respect that Lagos and Solana have achieved, and I feel honored to have them join this deliberation.

Nabil Fahmy, dean of the School of Global Affairs and Public Policy at the American University in Cairo, and Tosun Terzioğlu, the president of Sabanci University in Istanbul (with Tara Hopkins, founder of the Civic Involvement Program), have each contributed a chapter to this part. Minister Trevor Manuel of South Africa and Edgar Pieterse weigh in both thoughtfully and provocatively as well. These perspectives from diverse academic and geographical backgrounds have been indispensable to assessing the legitimacy and the feasibility of this global civics proposal.

The second part explores how to set up a formal global civics curriculum. There obviously can be many ways to have a thoughtful discussion about global civics. These chapters are meant to start this inquiry rather than to close it. In order to have a variety of perspectives, I have asked two colleagues, Graham Finlay of the University College Dublin and Vusi Gumede of the University of Johannesburg, to jointly develop a syllabus for a fourteen-week course. In addition, I asked Murat Belge of Bilgi University in Istanbul—a quintessential public intellectual—to put together a global civics reading list exclusively from works of literature. I myself set out to imagine a series of miniworkshops that would use documentaries and websites, as well as scholarly and literary works, to stimulate discussion about a global civics. These workshops are imagined as an alternative to the standard academic format and can be used both at academic and nonacademic settings by students and adults alike. If the reader is convinced of the utility, legitimacy, and feasibility of any of these approaches, she or he can use one or all of the three alternatives in conceiving a global civics forum.

This book and the overall project would not have been possible without the active involvement, encouragement, input, and support of Ayse Gul Altinay, Kemal Derviş, Ali Riza Gürsel, Lou Anne Jensen, Osman Kavala, the late Brooke Shearer, George Soros, and Strobe Talbott. The support and engagement of each of them were so crucial that the absence of even one would have precluded the existence of this volume and the overall project. I am grateful to all of them.

I feel fortunate to have worked throughout 2010 with five outstanding interns: Gorkem Aydemir, Cansu Ekmekcioglu, Mehmet Energin, Basak Otus, and Can Ozden. Their commitment to the project was invaluable. I am also grateful to the Jenesis Group and the Open Society Foundation for their generous grants in support of this publication and the Global Civics Project. Kristina Server, Mao-Lin Shen, and Janet Walker of Brookings have been cherished colleagues throughout this process. And Starr Belsky edited the chapters expeditiously.

We at Brookings see global civics as a long-term engagement and will proceed to establish a network of universities around the world that have made a normative and an organizational commitment to including global civics in their curricula. Many of the challenges faced by all of us are global; networks to think through and discuss appropriate responses need to be as well.

ONE

Why a Global Civics?

HAKAN ALTINAY

The broad manifestations of today's epic global interdependence are
well known. Financial engineering in the United States can determine
economic growth in every part of the world; carbon dioxide emissions
from China can affect crop yields and livelihoods in the Maldives, Bangladesh, Vietnam, and beyond; an epidemic in Vietnam or Mexico can
constrain public life in the United States; and volcanic ash from Iceland
disrupts travel across Europe. The inherent difficulties of devising and
implementing solutions to global problems through nation-states have
also become apparent. Traditionally, two broad models have been used
to deal with this predicament. The first relies on a wide range of creative
ad hoc alliances and solutions. When standard global public heath instruments proved insufficient, the Global Fund to Fight AIDs, Tuberculosis,
and Malaria was established. When the Internet became global, its management was turned over to ICANN (Internet Corporation for Assigned
Names and Numbers), which among other things enlists the input of
individual Internet users in its governance, a significant departure from
conventional intergovernmental multilateralism.

The second model is based on a more systematic reliance on rule of
international law and also on what is known as the global public goods
paradigm. Proponents of this concept point first and foremost to the
existence of certain vital global public goods, climate being the most

1

obvious example. The global public goods paradigm also implies some commensurability, if not uniformity, in the way people respond to various global collective action challenges. Some tend to feel suffocated by this expectation of commensurability among various global governance tracks; others find it reassuring and liberating. Many in the periphery have been largely absent from this debate, except for expressions of indignation about the unfairness of the status quo interspersed with acts of obstructionism.

Both of these models are premised on the belief that global governance is essentially a technocratic puzzle for which smart institutional design will provide the necessary answers. Yet, what the world is negotiating is, in effect, a global social contract, not a technocratic fix. The key question that needs to be answered is what responsibilities we all have toward people who happen not to be our compatriots. The question is so simple that one is often struck by the strange absence of ready answers to this fundamental question. Generating meaningful responses to this question will entail starting to imagine—without panic or rush, and with all the care and thoughtfulness this conversation requires—a global civics.

In its conventional use, "civics" refers to the familiar constellation of rights and responsibilities emanating from a social contract and citizenship in a nation-state. But what about *global* civics? Would this be feasible—or even desirable?

There are several plausible objections to the concept of global civics. One can argue that allowing for even a modest level of responsibility toward all the world's 6.9 billion people is so overwhelming that it is a nonstarter. Furthermore, it can be argued that any meaningful experience of pan-global consciousness and solidarity among human beings is nascent at best and therefore cannot form the basis for a formidable constellation of rights and responsibilities, and that the experience of being a global citizen is restricted to a few activists and international elites, like those who gather for the World Economic Forum in Davos. Finally, one can argue that civics assumes effective enforcement and a state, and since there is no world government, any talk of global civics is whimsical.

Notwithstanding such skepticism, I intend to demonstrate that it is, in fact, possible to imagine global civics. In attempting to do so, I first consider the unhelpful views that have impeded fruitful consideration of the concept of global civics. Then I outline the rationale for global civics and offer two thought experiments to operationalize this new concept.

Surrogate Debates

It is not surprising that there is skepticism about the concept of global civics because surrogate discussions about global civics have left much to be desired. Thus the case for global civics needs to begin by defusing several of these minefields.

The first minefield is formed by the group believing in *world federation by stealth*. Proponents of this view see each international problem as a way to get closer to some federal world government. They seem to be intent on delivering the good life through global structures since they doubt the legitimacy of nation-states and do not appreciate their ability to command allegiance and deliver results. They also have seemingly blind faith in international schemes and overlook the legitimate misgivings of those in many nation-states about turning over their sovereignty to woefully inadequate international institutions. The major negative consequence of this group's agenda is to raise diffuse suspicions about international frameworks and to scare reasonable people who might otherwise be open-minded about pragmatic international cooperation.

The second minefield is created by those who advocate *radical cosmopolitanism*. This argument, which is advanced by a small but influential group, posits that it is somehow morally reprehensible to care less about people halfway around the world than about one's own family and community. These radical cosmopolitans argue that we should be ready to give up all wealth until the last person in the world is not worse off than the rest of us. Critics have rightfully described advocates of these views as being interested in a hypothetical humanity while possessing a good deal of disdain for the actual fallible and imperfect humans themselves. Such morally virtuous cosmopolitans also underestimate how modern capitalism has improved the living standards of billions. They do not seem to care that preaching rarely works. Like the stance of the first group, this group's excessive demands intimidate reasonable people, who then resist any conversation about global normative frameworks.

The third minefield is laid by the *doomsday advocates*, a diffuse group of people who tend to think that tomorrow will be worse than today or yesterday. Often their scenarios of impending doom, unless some form of global cooperation is achieved immediately, are meant to spur people to action. However, these doomsayers do not seem to realize that crying wolf one too many times is unproductive. Nor do they appreciate the impressive progress made by humanity through piecemeal and pragmatic international cooperation schemes.[1] And even more important, they seem oblivious to the fact that fear is not a very potent motivator for the most important constituency for global cooperation: youth.

The fourth and final minefield is formed by the *cynical realists,* who readily argue that life is not fair and that one should grow up and not chase elusive and impractical global frameworks. Many of these cynics live in the advanced industrial countries, and they view all attempts at international cooperation with utter suspicion and are deeply skeptical about all national contributions—in treasure or in sovereignty—to global solutions. However, they underestimate both the need for proactive cooperation among many players to solve tomorrow's problems and the opportunity costs of such cynicism for that cooperation. These cynics also exist in the developing world, where they view any attempt to reform multilateral institutions as a plot to consolidate the power of the privileged few. They pontificate on the inherent unfairness of the status quo without any hint of what they might be prepared to do if they were to be convinced that a fairer order was within reach. Each group of cynics blames the unreasonableness of the other as the justification for their own position.

The Need for a Compass

The minefields laid by these four groups have made the initiation of a thoughtful conversation about global civics a forbidding task. Yet it will be next to impossible for the people living on Earth to navigate in a world of fast-growing interdependence if we do not at least begin to think about a global social contract. There is no reason to assume that interdependence will not continue or even accelerate in the near future. Many perceive that their ability to exercise meaningful control over their lives is eroding. This leads to anomie, anxiety, and a diffuse backlash. The choice is not between returning to the good old days of robust, nonporous borders and almighty nation-states versus being a helpless leaf at the mercy of winds from the far corners of the world. The choice is whether or not humanity will be able to hammer out a global social contract. A set of guiding principles—a moral compass—is needed to enable the people of the world to navigate the treacherous waters of unprecedented global interdependence.

One could think of it like driving a car. Each day millions of people drive at speeds above fifty miles an hour in a ton of metal extremely close to others who are doing the same thing. A slight move of the steering wheel in the wrong direction would wreak havoc, but we cruise carefree because we drive in an implicit fellowship with other drivers and have reasonable expectations about their behavior. Such fellowship with and expectations of other drivers, which serve to mitigate the theoretical risks of driving, can exist because people follow a long-established framework of laws, habits, and conventions about how to operate automobiles.

In an increasingly interdependent world, people need a corresponding global framework to put their minds at relative ease. Part of that reference framework must be based on global civics, a system of conscious responsibilities that we are ready to assume after due deliberation and corresponding rights that we are ready to claim. We all need to ask ourselves: to what responsibilities to other human beings are we personally ready to commit, and what would global civics look like? Two thought experiments can aid in figuring this out.

The Seven-Billionth Human Being

The first thought experiment for imagining the shape of global civics is to speculate about what one would say to welcome the seven-billionth human being, who will join the rest of us on this planet in 2012. A worthwhile exercise would be for each of us to take fifteen minutes out of our day to imagine what we would tell our fellow seven-billionth person about the human condition awaiting her or him. This conversation, however hypothetical, would help us take stock of the global situation that we have all helped produce. It would also set us on a path toward discovering our most imminent responsibilities to each other and the next generation—the essence of global civics.

The first thing we could tell our newcomer is that she can expect to live more than seventy years and that this is twice as long as what people counted on a century ago. We would tell this newcomer that though the world is a very unequal place in terms of income and wealth, disparities in life expectancy are decreasing. We could report in good conscience that the world possesses some effective global public health instruments, and that we have eradicated smallpox and might see the end of polio and malaria in her lifetime. She could be told to expect to have more than eleven years of schooling, education being another area where gross but diminishing global disparities loom large. We could also report that the world that awaits her prizes gender equality more than in any other era, so she can anticipate a more enabling world than her mother or grand-mother experienced.

In the spirit of first giving the good news, we can in good faith report that this seven-billionth person will have capabilities that not only empower her but would have been the envy of emperors and tycoons from earlier centuries. In terms of information and knowledge, our newcomer will have unprecedented access through the likes of Google Scholar, JSTOR (Journal Storage), and Wikipedia. The breadth of information and knowledge available and the ease of her access to such information would have been unfathomable to the *Encylopédistes* and academies of sciences of previous centuries.

At the same time, we should admit to her that there are critical risks. Although we know about the mind-numbing horrors of previous geno-cides and have resolutely sworn not to allow this ultimate crime to recur, the sad fact is that nobody would likely come to rescue our seven-billionth fellow human were she to face genocide. We would have to tell her that not only have the world's military powers abdicated their solemn responsibility to protect, but they have also not allowed the development of procedures and institutions for people to join a UN volunteer army to intervene in cases of imminent genocide.

We would also need to tell this newcomer that we have set into motion, first unknowingly and then with full awareness for the past twenty years, a chain of events related to climate change that may very soon become irreversible and lead to catastrophic environmental consequences. We now know that hydrocarbons are priced too low and do not reflect the real cost that their consumption inflicts on the environment and future generations. In effect, future generations have been subsidizing our current welfare, and they will need to deal with a deferred and compounded bill. We would need to note that while we were able to devise a plan for collective global action to prevent depletion of the ozone layer, a similar framework to mitigate climate change has thus far eluded us.

Finally, we would need to tell her that for decades in the twentieth century, the world's superpowers gambled with human civilization by amassing thousands of nuclear warheads, and that on more than one occasion, humanity was remarkably close to a nuclear holocaust. Although, as of today, we have not realized the forty-year-old goal of total nuclear disarmament enshrined in the Non-Proliferation Treaty, we have reduced the active nuclear arsenal to a fraction of what it once was.

Working on a welcome message for our seven-billionth fellow human being provides us with an opportunity for introspection as well as a frank accounting of the implicit responsibilities we have to other human beings and future generations, which constitute the very essence of global civics. Doing unto others what we would have them do unto us remains the most resilient benchmark for decent conduct in human history. This hypothetical conversation with our newcomer could set us on a path to answering some of these cardinal questions and help us elucidate what global civics would entail.

A Global Veil of Ignorance

In considering the shape of global civics, a second, more elaborate thought experiment is the global veil of ignorance, inspired by John Rawls and his book *A Theory of Justice*.[2] Rawls proposes thinking about justice both on procedural grounds and in terms of a particular definition: "justice as fairness." According to this definition, the organizing principles for a society would be agreed upon, hypothetically, in an initial position of equality, and these principles would end up governing all further agreements and the kinds of social cooperation and government that could be established. This situation would put people behind a "veil of ignorance," which would keep them from knowing their position in society or their fortune in the distribution of assets and abilities. The point of all this is to ensure that the organizing principles agreed to behind the veil of ignorance could not be designed to favor any particular condition, and that these principles would be the result of fair deliberation and agreement. Although Rawls's basic proposition is a familiar Kantian move, one can argue that all major philosophical and religious traditions have similar tenets. The maxim of treating others as we wish to be treated by them in commensurate situations is both a simple proposition and quite possibly one of the most radical ideas in history.[3]

So how would the world look behind a global veil of ignorance? For what key issues would we want to set rules behind this veil, and what would we leave to the actual business of life and politics after the veil is lifted? My hunch is that we would want to have rules for things that we are absolutely sure about and for vital risks that we would want to have meaningful guarantees against. Constituent features of a good life cannot be delivered through global structures. A good life has much more to do with camaraderie, friendship, family, and affection than global measures. Therefore, the global rules to be set behind the veil of ignorance would need to be minimal, not the result of a familiar temptation to engage in global social engineering and to deliver the good life through global governance. Furthermore, rules set behind the global veil of ignorance ought not to aim to replace politics. The majority of the issues we care about should and will remain the subject of national and local politics. A global veil of ignorance would simply help us identify those exceptional issues that we would want to regulate before engaging in the essential business of life and politics. And this, in turn, would provide invaluable insights into what needs to be encompassed by global civics.

Assuming that we are all present at the founding moment behind the global veil of ignorance, our first question as "founders" would be whether we would want a world government, a world federation, or opt for the nation-state as the primary unit of allegiance and international cooperation. From Kant to the World Federalist Movement, many have argued for a world parliament. If we were behind the veil, what would probably strike us is how little support movements like the World Federalists have had over the years. Manufactured or otherwise, allegiance to other people who speak our language and share a history and a territory with us seems to have survived the test of time. Therefore, as hypothetical founders behind the veil, we would likely opt to keep the nation-state, though I imagine we would also hope that nation-states would be more prone to cooperation than they are today. Even without the veil, global opinion surveys show that even in more unilateralist and sovereignist countries such as China, India, and the United States, more people support than oppose such multilateral notions as the UN's responsibility to protect and compliance with World Trade Organization (WTO) rulings, even against their own countries.[4]

The second vital question that founders can reasonably expect to confront is whether people would still want capitalism as the system of production and distribution. From the Luddites to the World Social Forum in Porto Alegre, various anticapitalist traditions have maintained that capitalism destroys more than it creates and leads to gross inequalities, which in turn rob humans of their dignity. Yet in the last two centuries, there has been a level of material prosperity totally unprecedented in human history. It is true that there are dramatic inequalities in the world: the world's richest 2 percent owns more than half of global assets.[5] This is unlikely to look very agreeable behind a global veil of ignorance. Yet we also know that the dramatic increase in income inequality between households is a result of the early industrialization process in the West and its immediate aftermath, from 1820 to 1950.[6] Inequality between households, though very high, has held steady and not increased further since 1950, even though there is a common impression that income inequality has been increasing in the world in the last few decades.[7] Increased communication and awareness of disparities may partially explain the difference between prevailing impressions and what various studies show. While income inequality has held steady for the last fifty years, we know that around the world, inequalities in years of schooling and disparities in life expectancy have both dramatically improved. The median human being today has far greater capabilities, as defined by Amartya Sen, available to him or her than did Genghis Khan or Napoleon.

Therefore, when founders review the evidence behind the global veil of ignorance, they are likely to be distressed by the size of income inequalities. However, they are even more likely to be impressed by the creative energies unleashed by capitalist modernity and thus would opt to keep the capitalist system while continuing to think and negotiate the appropriate mechanisms to reduce the negative externalities of these inequalities. Founders would probably be dismayed by the hubris displayed at the commanding heights of capitalism, but they might decide that these excesses would be better addressed through activism and politics rather than through any timeless rule to be set behind the veil of ignorance.

So far, I have suggested that the founders behind the global veil of ignorance are likely to keep the fundamentals the same. This could be an important revelation for the development of global civics. People sometimes treat the status quo as an arbitrary state of affairs that they need to tolerate and endure. Yet, if this experiment points toward the truth, the current status quo would also likely have been reached through a process of meritocratic deliberation.

However, not all issues are like that. For instance, if I were a founder behind a global veil of ignorance, I would want to institute much more effective guarantees against major risks such as climate change. Most simulations show that business as usual with respect to the climate will soon mean reaching the point of no return, triggering a chain reaction of events with catastrophic impacts on human existence and civilization on Earth. Yet the qualities of the underlying dynamics make climate change an especially difficult challenge. For instance, there is a gap of about thirty years between carbon emissions and the full consequences of those emissions. This long duration between cause and effect weakens motivation for behavioral change. For example, the fact that significant percentages of adults continue to smoke, despite proven health consequences, demonstrates that humans find it difficult to give up immediate gratification to avoid costs deferred thirty years into the future. Furthermore, even if half of the world's population practices prudence and restraint, the lack of cooperation by the other half may still preclude humanity's survival.

Given the high stakes and the difficult nature of the climate change problem, if I were a founder behind the global veil of ignorance, I would want a clear rule to be established. That rule would need to be based on the recognition of the equal rights of all human beings to emit carbon dioxide and other equivalents. This would require determining the maximum safe level for carbon dioxide and its equivalents, and dividing that level equally among 6.9 billion humans.[8] Those who want to emit more than their equal and safe share could do so only after establishing a sustainable, verifiable, and measurable sequestering scheme, or after receiving emission credits from others. Advanced societies could acquire emission credits through the provision of clean production, mitigation, and adoption technologies to others, but the basic rule could not be negotiated.[9] Given the dramatic adjustments that would entail for global economies, founders might choose to institutionalize a meaningful grace period where carbon intensity would be the benchmark instead of per capita emissions.

Humanity dared fate and gambled with its very existence through nuclear arms production for decades during the twentieth century. The contingency of a nuclear holocaust is likely to trigger a reaction among the founders behind the global veil of ignorance. The nuclear arsenals have been reduced in the last two decades, but the noble and rational goal of total nuclear disarmament that was central to the Nuclear Non-Proliferation Treaty has still not been realized. Founders are likely to insist on the swift realization of that goal.

A similar risk that those behind the global veil of ignorance are likely to seek guarantees against is genocide. Humans have frequently been subject to this ultimate crime, and the solemn responsibility to protect has equally frequently been abdicated for parochial reasons. This is unlikely to look acceptable behind a veil of ignorance. Thus founders might chose to strengthen the International Criminal Court (ICC), insisting that parties refusing to join the ICC lose some of their sovereign privileges, such as their seat at the UN General Assembly. Furthermore, the founders might seek to address the chronic understaffing of the UN military. This problem is a consequence of the nation-state being the primary unit of allegiance, for in accepting that, we also accept that citizens cannot be compelled to risk life and limb if there is no national interest. Yet national conscription is not the only option for fulfilling the responsibility to protect and to prevent genocide. People have often taken up arms in other countries for their beliefs. The International Brigades that fought in the Spanish Civil War are the most celebrated example, but the practice is older. Therefore the founders might direct the UN to implement a mechanism to accept volunteers for its army, ensure balanced representation from all global regions so that no particular group dominates the UN army during any given conflict, and train these soldiers to be disciplined during their mission, as there are too many examples of presumed rescuers harassing the very people they are meant to rescue. One can even imagine a setup where not just the UN Security Council but also the UN secretary general or a college of all former secretaries general could endorse a given mission, so that action would not be held hostage to veto by the five permanent members. Whatever risks might be associated with this iconoclastic system would pale in comparison to the opportunity cost of inaction when powerful military nations refuse to get involved in the face of imminent genocide.

One final fundamental issue that is likely to arise behind the global veil of ignorance is economic redistribution. Would the founders behind the global veil of ignorance feel compelled to set rules regarding redistribution, or would they leave this to the actual business of life and politics once the veil is lifted? I suspect that though the founders would likely find comfort in the decreases in some global disparities in recent decades, they would still feel uneasy about the overall size of the existing disparities. When reviewing the current tool kit for mitigating disparities, they would probably not be overly impressed by the track record of traditional overseas development assistance, though sui generis programs, such as the Global Fund to Fight AIDS, Tuberculosis, and Malaria, would likely command greater approval and acclaim. Founders also would likely be impressed by the effects of allowing people from poorer countries to reside and work temporarily in advanced economies. Remittances often act as greater multipliers than official development aid and uplift recipient communities more effectively. The issue of remittances and export of services through temporary migration comes under the WTO agenda, and the founders could assign this issue greater attention than it currently receives. However, given the mixed record of much global trade, development, and aid assistance, the founders behind the global veil of ignorance would probably institutionalize a review of disparities and various tools rather than be convinced of the timeless superiority of any one rule or tool.[10]

The point of these two thought experiments, of course, is not the brilliance or ineptitude of any particular set of results or answers but rather the process. My goal here is to show that there are some issues worth grappling with and that this is an inquiry worth pursuing. The similarities in what the two experiments reveal are telling: both experiments point to very analogous successes as well as to similar issues in need of imminent response.

Does Fairness Matter?

Skeptics still can insist that both thought experiments—and global civics in general—presuppose that fairness matters, whereas power, not fairness, matters both in life and in the world. These skeptics can find much in contemporary scholarship to support their perspective. These works frequently assert that all power is hard power and that being loved or respected is no substitute for being feared. The great-power game of nations always continues, they warn us, even when a higher goal or rhetoric is evoked. Superpowers are selfish, arbitrary, and dangerous nations, and they should not be embarrassed to be so or feel constrained by international legitimacy and laws.[11] They caution against assuming that the rise of the world's emerging powers is doing anything to the status of the United States as the sole superpower. Naturally, it would be folly to think that global public opinion is in effect a "second superpower," or even a crucial factor. Such concerns are like the Lilliputians binding an unsuspecting Gulliver. Anyone harboring such naive views needs to be told that good intentions are at best a distraction and a nuisance, and at worst a recipe for disaster, given their imprudence.[12] Cynics prefer to discount the achievements of transnational normative action, such as abolishing the slave trade or establishing the ICC.

Such cynical views are advanced not only from the hard power center of the international system but, in a fascinating twist, also from the various peripheries of the international system. The latter contingent argues that might makes right, which absolves those without formidable power of any responsibility for solving global problems or for even articulating their potential contributions if something other than the law of the jungle were to prevail. Thus the hubris of the powerful triggers irresponsibility among the not so powerful, which in turn is used by the cynics to argue the need for unadulterated power, given the rampant irresponsibility in the world at large.

I would argue fairness does matter today and will matter more in the future. The BRIC (Brazil, Russia, India, and China) and the Next 11 (Bangladesh, Egypt, Indonesia, Iran, Mexico, Nigeria, Pakistan, the Philippines, South Korea, Turkey, and Vietnam) groups of emerging nations are forecast to overtake the Group of Seven countries (Canada, France, Germany, Italy, Japan, United Kingdom, and United States). Though this change may not materialize for a very long time, and though such long-term projections are notoriously and predictably difficult, it is nevertheless evident that power disparities are less severe today and are likely to be even less so in the near future. At the same time, the current level of global interdependence and the very nature of the imminent global problems humanity faces have clear repercussions for the constellation of minimum alliances that are necessary to overcome these problems. Climate change is the most obvious case: unless all the major players *and their citizens* willingly and proactively cooperate, it is unlikely that human civilization as we currently know it will survive. It should be abundantly clear to all that a forceful Commodore Perry approach will not secure the proactive and willing cooperation of citizens around the world. Nor will hubris and cynicism encourage witnesses to speak out the next time they observe the plotting of an Abdul Qadeer Khan or an Osama bin Laden. Without a sense of fairness that appeals to many and a corresponding framework of global civics, humanity will not be able navigate the shoals generated by global interdependence and interconnectedness.

The world's architecture of power is not the only vector that is becoming more democratic. The rapid proliferation of transborder broadcasting has enabled us to become increasingly aware of each other's grief and bliss. We are not yet a global village, but we are significantly more aware of each other's predicaments than was the case a century or even a decade ago, and as a result, public opinion has come to matter even in the previously mandarin realm of foreign policy. It also so happens that public opinion around the world is more multilateralist than the views of policymakers. For instance, a recent survey by the organization World Public Opinion posed the choice between "Our nation should consistently follow international law; it is wrong to violate international law, just as it is wrong to violate laws within a country," and "If our government thinks it is not in our nation's interest, it should not feel obliged to abide by international laws." In the survey 57 percent of all the people from twenty-four countries chose compliance with international law and 35 percent chose national opting out.[13] Participants from countries that are often assumed to be unilateralist, such as China, India, and the United States, were in line with the global trend. Seventy-four percent of respondents in China, 49 percent in India, and 69 percent in the United States favored compliance with international laws, whereas 18 percent, 42 percent, and 29 percent, respectively, wanted national opt-outs.

The same survey also showed that people systematically underestimate to what a large extent their own multilateralist preferences are shared by their compatriots, and how alone they believe they are in their support for international law. Forty-eight percent of respondents indicated that compared to the average citizen, they personally were more supportive of consistently abiding by international law; 28 percent said they were less supportive. This "optical illusion" can possibly be explained by the hegemonic discourse of the cynics and may itself present an opportunity for enhanced multilateralism. Cynical policymakers, on the other hand, have a good deal of disdain for these popular preferences for international norms and complain, for example, that "Americans do not want their power raw; it has to be sautéed in the best of causes."[14] A similar survey has shown that 55 percent of the people in twenty-four countries wanted their governments to be more ready to act cooperatively to achieve mutual gain, as opposed to the 39 percent who felt that their governments tend to be too willing to compromise and are often taken advantage of.[15]

As power disparities further decrease in the future, and as larger alliances that are more based on societal preferences become necessary, notions and perceptions of fairness will be central to forging the requisite alliances, making global civics not only a constituent feature of decency but a central part of enlightened self-interest.

Vital Forums

The ideal venue for the conversation about global civics is the university campus. Global challenges, from climate change to nuclear proliferation, have a generational cleavage, and thus there is more at stake for twenty-year-olds than sixty-year-olds. The previous generation built its networks and assets during a time when nation-states reigned unchallenged. Yet twenty-year-olds must contend with a much more interdependent future, where their well-being depends in part on people who live and work in other countries. Universities offer a unique setting where young people can grapple with new and thorny issues and pursue interconnections beyond what first meets the eye. Furthermore, as a global middle class emerges, university populations are becoming more representative of the myriad points of view on our planet.[16]

Liberal arts education aims to equip students with the information and analytical tools to better exercise command over their lives. In a recent commencement speech, Bill Gates expressed dissatisfaction with his education at Harvard, asking why during his time there he did not learn about the vast amount of misery in the world.[17] We would not want future generations to tell us that their university experiences did not prepare them for life in an interdependent world. To be sure, students may well decide that they do not have any responsibilities toward those who are not their compatriots, but this ought to be their conscious, deliberate decision, not an implicit default option.

It also would be a gross mistake to pretend that arriving at a global social contract and a global civics is an easy pursuit with obvious answers. Some have tried to determine the maximum number of people with which one can have a trust-based relationship during a lifetime, and their estimates have coalesced around 150 and 200. Whatever that number is, it is bound to be significantly smaller than the actual number of people we are likely to interact with in our daily lives. If we are a little disoriented and feel thinly stretched, it is not because we are somehow lacking but rather because we are human. If we are a little overwhelmed by potentially being empathic with many more people, that is also perfectly understandable.

Nonetheless, given how interdependent our lives have become on this planet, we cannot avoid some sort of concerted effort to address both our responsibilities to each other on this Earth and our rights as members of the world community. Such responsibilities and rights would constitute the core issues of a global civics. If universities in the twenty-first century do not provide their students with the forums and tools to discuss and figure out what their responsibilities are to their fellow human beings, and to develop the requisite normative compass for navigating the treacherous waters of global interdependence, then they would be failing in their mission. It may just be that we can never reach a timeless consensus on the exact extent and form of our responsibilities toward each other. Even so, the process of inquiry and debate is bound to be highly beneficial, enlightening, and empowering.

Notes

1. For an audit of existing global governance schemes, see Hakan Altinay, "The State of Global Governance: An Audit," YaleGlobal (http://yaleglobal.yale.edu/about/altinay.jsp).

2. John Rawls, *A Theory of Justice*, rev. ed. (Belknap Press, Harvard University, 1999).

3. There are, of course, other writings by Rawls and other Rawlsians on these issues. For our purposes, the intricacies of that debate are not all that relevant. Two caveats should suffice: I find Rawls's methodology in *A Theory of Justice* much more interesting than that of his later work, *The Law of Peoples* (Harvard University Press, 2001). I also think that Rawls's veil of ignorance is too thick, namely, that he does not allow us to possess vital knowledge necessary for thoughtful deliberation. He allows us to know only very general facts about our society, not its economic or social level, culture, or civilization. This seems to me to be too limited and not even necessary for the justice-as-fairness principle to work. Under the global veil of ignorance, we should be allowed to know history—for example, to be able to judge various alternatives.

4. An April 2007 survey by World Public Opinion at the University of Maryland shows that pluralities of Chinese, Indians, and Americans support compliance with adverse WTO rulings as well as the UN's responsibility to authorize the use of military force to protect people from severe human rights violations, such as genocide, even against the will of the government committing such abuses. See "Publics around the World Say UN Has Responsibility to Protect against Genocide," April 4, 2007 (www.worldpublicopinion.org/pipa/articles/btjustice human_rightsra/340.php?lb=bthr&pnt=340&nid=&id=); "World Public Favors Globalization and Trade but Wants to Protect Environment and Jobs," April 27, 2007 (www.worldpublicopinion.org/pipa/articles/btglobalizationtradera/349.php?nid=&id=&pnt=349&lb=btgl).

5. See James B. Davies and others, "The World Distribution of Household Wealth," Discussion Paper, World Institute for Development Economics Research, United Nations University, 2008 (www.wider.unu.edu/stc/repec/pdfs/rp2008/dp2008-03.pdf). The same study estimates the global wealth Gini coefficient as 0.892. The Boston Consulting Group's *Global Wealth 2010* report estimates that 0.1 percent of global households have 21 percent of global wealth, and 0.8 percent of global households own 38 percent of global assets. See Jorge Becerra and others, *Global Wealth 2010: Regaining Lost Ground: Resurgent Markets and New Opportunities* (Boston Consulting Group, June 2010). In terms of income, the top 10 percent is estimated to get half of global income. See Branko Milanovic, "Global Income Inequality: What It Is and Why It Matters," Working Paper, UN Department of Economic and Social Affairs, 2006 (www.un.org/esa/desa/papers/2006/wp26_2006.pdf). In chapter 4 of this volume, Trevor Manuel and Edgar Pieterse rightfully ask whether there is any level of inequality that human society may find unacceptable.

6. See table 11.1, "World Inequality in Historical Perspective," in Branko Milanovic, *Worlds Apart: Measuring International Global Inequality* (Princeton University Press, 2005), p. 142.

7. Income inequality between countries has continued to increase since 1950. Income inequality within individual countries has also increased in the case of several countries. Yet inequality between all the households in the world has not increased, and this is likely to be the key indicator that the founders behind the global veil of ignorance would follow most attentively.

8. While this formula of equal per capita emissions may initially seem far fetched, German Chancellor Angela Merkel and the Indian government have used it in the past. See http://yaleglobal.yale.edu/content/merkel-leads-climate-change.

9. Although the issue of intergenerational and international burden sharing receives most of the attention, the issue of technological advance is even more important. Capping average temperature increase at 2 degrees Celsius would require decreasing global emissions from their current annual level of about forty gigatons of CO_2 equivalents down to twenty gigatons. This would need to happen at a time of continued population and economic growth, and cannot be achieved without multiple technological breakthroughs.

10. For a recent review of available policy options, see Jessica Cohen and William Easterly, *What Works in Development: Thinking Big and Thinking Small* (Brookings, 2009). For an interesting methodology for assessing options—albeit with disappointing results—see Bjorn Lomborg, *Global Crises, Global Solutions* (Cambridge University Press, 2004).

11. Robert Kagan makes an unabashed defense of this argument in *Dangerous Nation* (New York: Alfred A. Knopf, 2006).

12. For examples of dismissive treatment of transnational movements, see two articles by Walter Russell Mead, "The Death of Global Warming," *American Interest Online*, February 1, 2010 (http://blogs.the-american-interest.com/wrm/2010/02/01/the-death-of-global-warming), and "Blowing Hot and Cold," *American Interest Online*, October 17, 2009 (http://blogs.the-american-interest.com/wrm/2009/10/17/blowing-hot-and-cold).However, not everyone is so dismissive of transnational movements. The National Intelligence Council has considered a scenario where nongovernmental organizations increase in number and strength due to the capacity of individuals and groups to affiliate with each other via the Internet, and consequently UN member states feel compelled to allocate to nongovernmental organizations twenty seats at the UN General Assembly with the same voting rights as nation-states. See National Intelligence Council, *Global Trends 2025* (U.S. Government Printing Office, 2008), p. 91.

13. World Public Opinion, "World Public Opinion on International Law and the World Court," November 2009 (www.worldpublicopinion.org/pipa/pdf/nov09/WPO_IntlLaw_Nov09_quaire.pdf).

14. Leslie Gelb, *Power Rules* (New York: HarperCollins, 2009), p. 72. In this book that purports to rescue American foreign policy, there is an astonishing and total neglect of the climate change issue.

15. World Public Opinion, "World Public Opinion on International Cooperation," December 2009 (www.worldpublicopinion.org/pipa/pdf/dec09/WPO_Cooperation_Dec09_quaire.pdf).

16. A recent Brookings study forecasts the global middle class increasing from 1.8 billion in 2010 to 5 billion in 2030. See Homi Kharas and Geoffrey Gertz, "The New Global Middle Class : A Cross-Over from West to East," March 2010 (www.brookings.edu/~/media/Files/rc/papers/2010/03_china_middle_class_kharas/03_china_middle_class_kharas.pdf).

17. Bill and Melinda Gates Foundation, "Bill Gates—2007 Harvard Commencement," June 6, 2007 (www.gatesfoundation.org/speeches-commentary/Pages/bill-gates-2007-harvard-commencement.aspx).

PART I

Global Perspectives

TWO

Ten Perspectives on Global Civics

HAKAN ALTINAY
with Balveer Arora, Jonathan Fanton, David Held,
Andrey Kortunov, Ivan Krastev, Ricardo Lagos,
Thomas Pogge, Dani Rodrik, Dingli Shen, and Javier Solana

I n the following series of dialogues, ten internationally respected scholars and leaders are each interviewed in an attempt to ascertain what
the global challenges are that face the world today and the role of global
civics in helping humanity address these challenges. The interviewees
represent several nationalities and disciplines, and as such they bring a
diversity and wealth of perspectives to this exchange of ideas.

Questions are shown in italics, followed by the interviewee's initials
and response.

BALVEER ARORA, *professor of political science and former rector*
of Jawaharlal Nehru University, New Delhi

Do we really need a conversation about global civics?
BA: The exercise that you are engaged in is a very significant and important one. I am convinced that a global civics built on the foundations of a
shared sense of responsibility and global solidarity, and on a fundamental
respect for human dignity and human rights, makes a great deal of sense.

We need to imagine new forms of global governance. Civil society
groups and citizens who share a sense of global civics will end up play-
ing a greater role in shaping the future forms of global governance. We
will not have one world government, but governance of global problems

will have to be grounded in shared values. These values will be reached through a process where we take each other seriously.

Do you think fairness matters? Some have argued that only power matters.
BA: Power of course matters, but power without a sense of equity and justice would be immoral. Fairness in the sense of equity and justice is indispensable for power and for global governance in order to achieve moral legitimacy.

Is there a role for civil society or for universities in all this?
BA: What is possible today was not possible fifty—or even twenty—years ago. This is a moment where many more things are possible. The context of global governance has changed, the extent of our connectivity has changed, and our consciousness has changed. Therefore the possibilities of today are much greater than before.

Civil society organizations are the foremost actor. They organize the citizens and build a common civic consciousness and solidarity. They have an increasing role to play in thinking about and acting on our global challenges; they already play a crucial role in some of these fields. Civil society organizations have played a significant role in the case of the Millennium Development Goals, in particular with regard to the eradication of extreme poverty, achieving universal primary education, and promoting gender equality. These are tangible issues where global civics would play itself out through a sense of solidarity.

As far as universities are concerned, they are the places where knowledge is generated and transmitted. They are where young people are equipped with the tools they need to face the challenges of the contemporary world and of their lives. Universities have to expose their students to the ideas and values needed for an interdependent world. Theirs is a crucial role.

How would something like global civics be received at Jawaharlal Nehru University and other Indian universities?
BA: I think global civics, human rights, human dignity, distinct yet overlapping cultural identities, and the need for reciprocal knowledge should be a part of the university curriculum. These notions have to be taught as

a part of what it means to be living in a globalized, interdependent world. Global civics and fairness is less a reality and more a goal that we should aspire to and teach about.

The potential of a permanent Indian seat at the United Nations Security Council also provides an added impetus. Through this process young people have become sensitized to the importance of the United Nations and its agencies.

What should go into the global civics curriculum?
BA: Basic texts that stress the unity of mankind should be a key part of the curriculum. The importance of human dignity, of accommodation and tolerance, and of advancing reciprocal knowledge is also key. You invoke *vasudheva kutumbakam,* which means that the whole world is one family; Gandhi invoked these values as well as equity and justice. The unity of humanity, a common destiny, and shared values binding mankind have been taken up by many other philosophical and religious traditions. Global civics teaching will need to be grounded in diverse local traditions and narratives. I know your book will include a discussion of how to use literature in teaching and discussing global civics, and I think that is an excellent idea. Tolstoy and Dostoyevsky, as well as several other authors, have given us seminal texts to discuss these issues. A global civics curriculum should make use of these vital works.

JONATHAN FANTON, *former president of the John D. and Catherine T. MacArthur Foundation, Chicago, and of the New School for Social Research, New York*

Is global civics a necessity? A luxury? A distraction?
JF: I think it is very much a core necessity for a world that is more just, peaceful, and humane. I really do believe that you have made a very strong case for it.

We need a global civics because of our increasing global interdependence?
JF: There is no question the current path of history is making all of us more interdependent. The challenge is to develop and nurture a global civics without losing a sense of space and identity, and I am optimistic

that it can be done. Technology is one broad area that is bringing us together, crossing boundaries, and intertwining our fates. You mention climate change and nuclear disarmament; they both force us into a global conversation and global solutions, without which we are putting the future of the human race at risk.

What should be our posture going into that global conversation? Some argue that all power is hard power and that we should not be overly concerned by legitimacy and global public opinion.

JF: What I like about the way you pose these questions is the way you invite a paradigm shift. In some ways the language of hard power and soft power is the old paradigm, but the new paradigm is not immediately apparent. However, I think what you are engaged in is path breaking and path setting in posing these questions and provoking us to think big and fresh.

Is there a role for universities in all this?

JF: I believe that the argument you make about universities being an indispensable forum for thinking through our responsibilities to citizens of other countries is a powerful one. I am familiar with Project Pericles, which works with liberal arts colleges to develop civics courses and internships. After a modest beginning, it has become a movement across the United States. I can envision a similar trajectory for the global civics idea.

What do you see when you review the general landscape of higher education in the United States and across the world?

JF: I see a couple of challenges for American higher education. First, it is expensive. International students have been subsidizing the cost of higher education in America for quite some time. As high-quality higher education becomes more available around the world, the American model will be difficult to sustain. Also, the current generation of students grew up searching and finding information on the Internet. Print media were slow to react to this change, and I fear higher education may be equally slow in coming to terms with the full extent of the technological changes. I also have seen the political will and capacity to reform and upgrade higher education in places like Nigeria and Russia. I can testify that the appetite for the sort of thing you are talking about is very much there.

What about foundations? Is there a role for them?

JF: Let me first give an example and then draw a lesson. The MacArthur Foundation took an interest in the way that professionals working in the field of development were trained. The foundation assembled a commission headed by Jeffrey Sachs and having international membership. The International Commission on Education for Sustainable Development Practice held hearings all over the world, and at the end advised that the disciplines of science, engineering, management, and health should be given a much larger role in the training of development professionals. Political science and economics used to be the main pillars of the development curriculum. The commission also argued the need for a deep internship experience, where students spend a summer or a semester in the field. The core course is web based and is available all around the world. MacArthur also funded a dozen demonstration projects around the world. Many other institutions have signed on and have adopted the changes advocated. This is a recent example of how a foundation can turn a good idea into a reality.

Foundations can do a great deal of good if they work on an idea whose time has come. They can be ahead of the curve and identify imminent needs. They can and should use their resources to seize on these needs and develop appropriate responses. The right timing is essential. Foundations should also support the demonstration phase as well. They really can galvanize profound change.

Does fairness matter?

JF: I believe strongly that it does. The opinion polls that you cite correspond with what we saw at MacArthur when we supported a poll by the Chicago Council on Global Affairs to see what people thought about the International Criminal Court (ICC). The poll found that almost 70 percent of ordinary Americans support the ICC and think that the United States should be party to it. When you pose the same question to political leaders, not only do you get a lower percentage of support, but they also underestimate the appetite of ordinary Americans for things like the ICC.

If you were asked to develop a global civics curriculum, are there things you would consider sine qua non?

JF: Well, you mention John Rawls, and he would be in my curriculum as well. I would want core reading of theory and philosophy but not just

Western authors, and assessments of the history and universality of these ideals. I would want to see a section on practical problems that require global action—climate change, human rights, global public health, and the like. I would also want to see an electronic component where students across national boundaries work on similar questions. There could be a few courses taught globally. There should also be opportunities for face-to-face conversations, through internships and videoconferencing.

DAVID HELD, *professor of political science and codirector of Global Governance, London School of Economics*

Do you think we need a conversation about our rights and responsibilities as human beings and fellow residents of the planet?

DH: I think we do. We live surrounded by a very pressing conjunction of forces and processes of change. The first of these is that the West has written the rules of the global interaction for the last 300 years but will increasingly be unable to do so. The world is shifting toward multipolarity, prompted by the rise of Asia. And just at this moment of shifting global power, there is also growing acknowledgment that the UN systems founded in 1945, to put it bluntly, are no longer fit for their purposes. The UN system was designed and anchored in a far different era, with different conditions and a different power structure. Finally, all this is occurring at a time when some of the global challenges are becoming most dangerous. Climate change, the reform of global financial powers, nuclear proliferation, and the future of global trade negotiations are cases in point. So the world's power alignments are shifting precisely at a moment when the traditional global institutions have become weak and vulnerable.

This is both a dangerous moment and a great opportunity. People have tended to assign formulaic responses to these problems. One was to say that the markets know best, to hope that the markets will generate solutions to collective action problems, and to defer to the markets. Given the record of the last thirty years, my judgment would be that the markets have singularly failed. They create externalities, and they need regulation and policing. Competition requires cooperation to achieve the flourishing of public goods.

Another way of responding to global problems has been to create multilateral clubs. Take the Basel Committee, which is supposed to deal with the issues of the international financial system. Though it is dominated by a small group of Western banking powers, its policies generalize risk management across the world. The committee's model affects everyone, but that model has been shaped according to the members' own narrow interests, and the result has been, eventually, the global financial crisis.

I do not think these tasks should be left to the market or to the clubs. In my view what has failed at the global level is nondemocracy. What are the other alternatives? One is a return to the naked geopolitical power struggle. We live in a moment of the rise of new great powers, India and China, and the attendant rush for resources can lead to an explosion in geostrategic competition. But surely geostrategic competition cannot be the solution to our global problems. All this leads me to conclude that "realism" as we have known it is dead, and cosmopolitanism is the new realism. In that sense, this is indeed the time to talk about values and to create a new global deal.

What is the appropriate posture for starting the conversation?
DH: There was Pax Britannica in the nineteenth century and Pax Americana in the twentieth century, but in this century there is no pax anything as yet. The old global powers have lost the ability to write the rules, and the new global powers do not have the ability to take up the challenge and the responsibility. This creates the space for the dialogue that you and I want. Of course, countries like China, India, and Russia bring with them different resources and histories to the discussion table. None of these actors are yet full parties to the cosmopolitan project, but at least in China, there are lively debates at universities about these issues and other pressing global problems.

We also do not start from nowhere: the twentieth century did provide significant stepping-stones. During the preceding century, laws of war and human rights laws were developed that circumscribe power in significant ways. Europe modeled a way to pool sovereignty, and a global civil society began to flourish across the world. And now we see the emergence of civil society–rooted global citizenship. In addition, global public opinion is also beginning to emerge; in fact there are now several surveys that track global public opinion on key issues.

What about the European Union and its role?
DH: For Europe the end of the cold war was a victory and a curse at the same time. The march of communism was eliminated as a threat, but it turns out that the project of European integration was receiving a good deal of push from the threat of communist takeover, and once that threat was gone, some of the motivation that bound Europe together weakened. There has been a resurgence of old European jealousies and rivalries. The region now faces a set of difficult challenges, for Europe suffers the most from the changing balance of global economic power. The position of the United States is fairly static, Asia is on the rise, and Europe is declining. The future of the euro itself is in doubt.

However, Europe also has some assets. It is home to the most interesting global governance experiment of the last fifty years. Europe has demonstrated how antagonistic powers can pool sovereignty to create a Kantian zone of peace. Though Europe has the normative model, it has not been able to project its power because old European national jealousies are still intact. Do I think Europe should be at the table helping shape the next set of rules? Yes. Do I think it will be able to? No.

And the other side of the Atlantic?
DH: Having just come back from Washington, I am struck by how self-enclosed and self-preoccupied the United States is. The view of the world in the United States is very parochial. Even the Left is preoccupied about how to interpret American interests rather than promoting a wider program.

Should universities be the venue where we discuss our rights and responsibilities toward each other?
DH: My view is that this is a vital part of the education of all young people. We need not wait till university; we can begin to discuss this in primary school. In the past we all had to color the map of the world with different colors for each country. After the NASA missions and satellite images of our planet, people have a newer conception of the world as a unified green-blue sphere. I find that younger children understand

connectivity very well, and they have an intuitive sense of fairness. All good teachers know how to get a discussion going on these issues with their students. Given that our current institutions are incapable of dealing with these global interrelations and frailties, the younger generation has to be engaged to address the upcoming challenges. Therefore, while global civics should be a part of the university curriculum, I would go further and say that these issues should be part of the civics curriculum everywhere, from ages five to twenty-one.

ANDREY KORTUNOV, *president of the New Eurasia Foundation, Moscow*

I argue that our increasing global interdependence necessitates a conversation about our responsibilities toward each other, something like a global civics. Is that really necessary? Why not continue on the current path?

AK: We can certainly pretend that the current system of global politics is ideal and that we do not need to change anything, but the odds are that if we continue to operate the way we have all along, we will face more and more crises, such as the global financial crisis and even security crises in the conventional sense. An examination of international relations during the last two to three decades will show that we have been accumulating problems without any solutions that can be considered final. Africa, the Middle East, the Balkans, and the Caucasus are cases in point.

Climate change strikes me as one of the most emblematic examples of our global interdependence, and as such is an issue that calls for a global civics perspective.

AK: I agree that climate change cannot be treated as a normal transaction between nation-states. Whether we manage to contain the worst consequences of climate change will depend in large part how each and every one of us will behave. State-centered approaches will not get us to the solution. A major deficiency of the current state-centered realist paradigm is its exclusive reliance on interests. The future of international relations is more likely to be defined by international regimes and the underlying norms. These norms are not an exclusive purview of the state but concern many nonstate actors.

Are these widely shared views in Russia?

AK: Twenty-five years ago Russia was obsessed with an idealistic vision of global politics. Gorbachev embodied the normative approach to global affairs. The dominant thinking was that communism should be replaced by a new normative framework that united the whole of humanity in a nonconfrontational world. But the reality—especially foreign policy actions by the United States—did not support this view. As a result these ideals were discredited to a large extent in the eyes of the people and especially the political elite. The political elite say, "We tried values. They were not embraced by the rest of the world. Now we pursue our interests."

Does this mean that the case for a normative approach is irreversibly damaged?

AK: Nothing is irreversible unless we are resigned to its being irreversible. There are serious changes occurring in Russia with regard to how people think about themselves and the world. Russia is becoming more integrated with the outside world. More people travel, study, and work abroad. Borders are becoming more porous. The Internet is a fast-growing phenomenon. One can think of Russia as an iceberg: the top is being exposed to all the frosty winds of international conflict and the harsh clash of interests, so the tip of the iceberg is frozen and apparently immobile; but the bulk of the iceberg under water is being melted by the currents of globalization and integration. The center of gravity is changing, and at some point the whole structure may flip and turn upside down.

Ultimately we will need to confront the fact that we cannot conceive of interests if we do not address values. We will need to rehabilitate the idea of values, and something like global civics and global responsibility will be a central part of that value system.

Is there a role for universities in thinking through these issues?

AK: Well, changing universities has been compared to moving a graveyard: it is an expensive and dirty process, and you do not get much help from the inside. Having said that, I see in Russia a greater acceptance of the social functions of higher education, both in the society and within universities. There is a greater appreciation that universities should not just produce graduates but also thoughtful citizens. The ethos of individual university management plays a significant role in all this.

If Russian universities called you up and asked for a global civics curriculum, what would you advise them to include in the curriculum?
AK: First of all, I would want to make sure that the historical background of global responsibility and global citizenship was surveyed. These concepts are not the exclusive preserve of Western liberals but have a long and noble trajectory in many traditions and geographies. We should not forget that we are not starting from scratch, that we stand on solid and diverse foundations and traditions. I also would want to see a critical discussion of the current mainstream thinking based on interests, nation-states, and short-term growth. Then we would need to apply the global civics perspective to a few specific problems. Finally, some hands-on practical service learning would be useful. It can start with a list of organizations and movements where students can do internships. Students need to see that this is not just the preoccupation of some eccentric visionaries but rather a preview of what is to come and quite possibly the central question of their adult lives.

I also like your proposal for addressing the seven-billionth person. These sorts of questions and projects would provoke students to think outside the box.

Does fairness matter?
AK: I think humans are significantly less cynical than is generally assumed. We all have a good deal of idealism but feel we need to hide it under a facade of cynicism. Tapping into that hidden idealism could trigger astonishing results.

IVAN KRASTEV, *chairman of the Center for Liberal Strategies, Sofia*

The story of our epic interdependence is well known but appropriate responses to that interdependence are less clear. What do we do?
IK: Managing interdependence is the key issue of our time. In the past there was the option to reverse interdependence. For example after World War I, there was a retreat in terms of globalization and interdependence.

But the current constellation of technological advances makes reversing global interdependence inconceivable. For a while people had an essentially positive outlook on interdependence. Interdependence was good news! However, lately there seems to be more fear about interdependence. This is true for individuals, elites, and states. The fact that their control over things is diminishing scares people. One manifestation of this is a proliferation of conspiratorial thinking.

In 1990–91 the communist system had lost its legitimacy, and nothing of substance was discussed in the parliament. All important issues were being discussed in the roundtable talks. The current Group of Twenty reminds me of that moment. It is like the meeting of emperors at the end of the nineteenth century. It is very informal, self-selecting, and has no enforcement mechanism, and yet it is perceived as highly legitimate. The more we talk about global architecture, the more informal our decision-making seems to become.

The publics are missing from all this. As a twisted result of globalization, publics are becoming more local. Thirty years ago when migrants arrived at their destination, they essentially would be cut off from their home countries. The newspapers from native countries would come late and infrequently, and they would rely on the newspaper of the host country. Today, with the Internet and satellite television, new immigrants can access their old sources and live in an informational ghetto. Despite the appearance of opening, we have in fact the closing of minds. This is not unrelated to the overall anxiety.

The 2008 book *The Big Sort* depicts graphically how thirty years ago a majority of Americans lived in counties with pluralistic political constellations, whereas now 70 percent live in counties where one of the two political parties wins in a landslide.[1] This exemplifies a trend where people are decreasingly exposed to difference.

So, what do we do?
IK: We all have to decide that the process of getting to know "the other" is the only way for us to deal with our anxieties. We have been overly concerned about reforms from above, for example, reform of the UN Security Council. I do not think that the world will be perceived as more fair or inclusive if the Security Council expands. I agree with you that

the answer does not lie within the institutional architecture. However, we do need a genuine conversation about the aspirations of "the other." We also need a conversation, as you suggest, about our responsibilities toward each other.

Where should this conversation take place? On the Internet? At universities? Through big public debates?
IK: Everywhere! At the end of the day, civil society requires trusting and engaging with strangers. The conversations should take place at different venues and in different languages.

I have a strong faith in debate and face-to-face conversation because this is the only real way that people can change their minds. The real intellectual hero of our time is not someone who defends a fixed position despite all odds but rather someone who can change his or her mind when faced with a better argument or data. Now it just so happens that the person who can change your mind is someone from your group. So dissidents, people who are willing to differ from the positions of their groups, are vital. The Internet seems to have become a debate forum where you only discuss with like-minded people. So no dissidents on the Internet.

In general, national civics education has been a success, and universities now should take up the global civics curriculum. In each country the debate and the curriculum would be different, but all participants should be cognizant that the process is part of a global movement.

What would you want to see in a global civics curriculum?
IK: I think we need to better understand the roots of transnational normative movements such as the antislavery movement. Most of the members of the antislavery movement were not former slaves; their motivation came from a sense of global solidarity and empathy. Lynn Hunt argues that the sensational novels of the eighteenth century were a vital incubator for the notion of human rights.[2] In these novels an aristocrat would empathize with the fate of the servant girl, making empathy across hierarchies conceivable. The moment you can identify with any other human being, you have the idea of humanity. I give this example because I feel we need to better understand the emotive side of this phenomenon. I have been interested in the personal stories of people who decided to

defend other people's rights, and I find that a powerful anecdote from a peer is almost always part of that transformation. A compelling story is more effective than a general theory of justice. So I hope the global civics curriculum takes into account the power of a well-told story.

Do you sense different responses to the idea of global civics across regions?

IK: Of course. Russians lost their universalist ambitions with the end of communism. They do not want to remake the world any more. Russian society today is very mistrustful; the events of the early 1990s have colored their perception of the international order. The Russia of today both wants to be a part of the world and also to protect itself from the world.

Europe believes that it is the model for the future of the world. Yet Europe may also end up on the periphery for the first time in 300 years. Europe cannot take its economic might for granted. Some of its strengths are in high culture, but interest in high culture is in decline across the world. What looked universal yesterday looks exceptional today. Europe is very secular, but no one else really is. Europe is also postsovereignist, but no one else is as comfortable with postsovereignty as Europe is. How to have effective multilateralism without European-style postsovereignism is a huge intellectual puzzle.

As for new powers, such as India and China, they should be encouraged to seek glory in their moral superiority. They should compete in terms of fairness. Their aspiration to be moral leaders is a beneficial dynamic for the world.

RICARDO LAGOS, *former president of Chile and former president of the Club of Madrid*

Do we really need a conversation about global civics?

RL: I think having a conversation about global civics is a definite necessity. It is absolutely fair to argue that our increasing interdependence requires us to consider a global civics. When you are a small country seeking development and using the world as a means to your development, then you conclude that some rules have to exist at the global level. It is not possible to have a globalized world without rules. However, it would be a pity to have a world where some would be the globalizers and others have to accept being globalized. The question is how to find a way to form what you call a global social contract.

How do we get to that global social contract?
RL: I was struck by the difference between the societal responses in South Africa and Spain versus those in India, as depicted in your paper *Does Fairness Matter?*[3] It is understandable that given their own national experience, peoples' reactions to the international community in South Africa and Spain are positive and optimistic. India, on the other hand, demonstrates a more nationalist approach given its experience of decolonization. National experiences with the international community are key to how countries act in taking on global responsibilities and contributing to the solution of global problems.

So societies are key to the global social contract?
RL: Yes. For instance, the world is experiencing the development and proliferation of citizens' organizations that share similar views, regardless of where they are, and they work around similar ideals across national borders. Climate change is a case in point. There are many organizations in all countries that feel a global solution is needed to a global problem.

   We live in a world with several problems that no single country can solve on its own. At the same time, we know that there are some problems where a few key countries must be involved. In the case of climate change, the solution has to include China and the United States. So we need to be idealistic and realistic at the same time.

Shuttling between the ideal and the feasible is indeed tricky. You were faced with that predicament in 2003 at the UN Security Council and the issue of using force in Iraq.
RL: The United States is one of Chile's main trading partners, and in 2003 we were working on a free trade agreement with the United States. But we were also not convinced that all diplomatic options were exhausted in the case of Iraq. Therefore we did not agree with our American friends at the UN Security Council. In this context I hope Chile's conduct in 2003 can be a source of hope for the world.

Trade is trade. A free trade agreement is about trade; it is not a political or a strategic treaty. Countries like Chile need robust rules at the global level. Rules cannot exist without multilateral organizations, and I was determined not to do anything that would undermine the multilateral institutions. For that reason, among others, Chile sent 300 hundred soldiers in less than seventy-two hours to the UN Stabilization Mission in Haiti, which the Security Council unanimously approved in February 2004.

Can we imagine a world where Chile and others go beyond being benign custodians of the multilateral institutions and advance the global norms by acting as global norm entrepreneurs?
RL: I hope and believe that this is possible. This is where civic organizations are so vital. Governments tend to be more constrained, whereas civic organizations have more freedom to act. The citizens' organizations are the basis of soft power. The initiative will come from them.

As the head of the Club of Madrid, you have taken the pulse of very different parts of the world. How will something like global civics be received in different parts of the world?
RL: I sense a great deal of sympathy and support for something like a global civics across Latin America and even in Brazil, which is an emerging power. The big powers may be more difficult to convince. We need to tell them that history demonstrates that no great power is permanent. Therefore they should contribute to the making of rules that they would be comfortable with when they are no longer members of the topmost tier. This kind of mind-set can be useful.

It is interesting that we went from the Group of Eight to the Group of Twenty in the last crisis. This expansion is an implicit endorsement of the changing nature of the global power architecture and the need to be more inclusive. It also opens up interesting possibilities for the civic organizations working on global issues.

What other trends do you observe?
RL: Technology is the new frontier. In our twenty-first-century societies, the relationship between citizens and political leaders has been transformed. Traditionally, newspapers have been indispensable for a

functioning democracy, and new information technologies will be equally transformative for today's political system.

At my foundation, Fundación Democracia y Desarrollo, we have a program called the Fifth Power where politicians can make statements or submit articles, but they need to be ready to answer any online comments they receive from the citizens. This is not a return to the Athenian agora, but for the first time in modern history, citizens are listened to one by one. It is much more important to create forums of this kind internationally. The Internet diminishes distances and fosters a global civics.

Maybe we can debate our message to the seven-billionth person, or we can ask people how they would act if they were the speechwriter for the next UN secretary general?
RL: That would be very interesting and useful.

Do universities have a role or a responsibility in helping us think about global civics?
RL: Human beings have always needed an institution for thinking about society at large and the future. In ancient times priests fulfilled that role, but for the last several centuries in the West that institution has been the university. It is essential for the universities to foster thinking about the increasingly interdependent world. Questions of global civics are their domain.

What should go into the global civics curriculum?
RL: We have to learn to think the other way around, counterfactually, iconoclastically. For example, can we not have the South Pole at the top of the world map, and the North Pole at the bottom? Imagine how different the world would look and its implications if we were to do that. The same holds true in the teaching of history: our history teaching can be centered around Europe or, say, China. We need to learn to approach global problems not through our narrow national backgrounds and instead adopt a new outlook. It is easy and comfortable to continue to rely on our national tool kits, but we need to be genuinely curious about the perspectives of others if we are serious about implementing a global civics.

THOMAS POGGE, *professor of philosophy and international affairs,*
Yale University

I propose that our current level of interdependence requires us to
go beyond conventional global governance and have a parallel
conversation about our responsibilities toward each other, a
conversation that I hope will lead to a global civics. Does this
strike you as sensible or whimsical or far-fetched?

TP: It strikes me as just right. I see two interrelated and deep structural problems in the present situation, which make what you propose an important move. Both of these problems relate to regulatory capture. There are a number of problems whose solutions transcend the national state, so countries get together and treaties are shaped. Given the emerging global architecture, rules are being generated rather rapidly on several fronts. The negotiating positions of the participating governments are shaped by their strongest domestic constituencies. Governments try to please those economic sectors likely to be affected most by these rules. Thus the German government's position will be greatly influenced by the country's largest export firms in the case of international trade, and by the big banks in the case of international financial regulations. Ordinary people will also be affected greatly by these rules, but their ability to participate in shaping these negations is severely limited. The nontransparent manner in which these negotiations take place is the most important impediment to greater participation. The media almost never provide sufficient information on these negotiations, and ordinary people lack the lobbying power. It is very rare for trade unions or big nongovernmental organizations to learn and understand what is going on in real time, and to have the opportunity to weigh in. So there are a very small number of players making the rules. Consequently there is regulatory capture. The paradigm example of this is the Agreement on Trade-Related Aspects of Intellectual Property Rights (TRIPS agreement), where four industries— pharmaceuticals, software, entertainment, and agrobusiness—lobbied very heavily the right governments, those of the European Union and the United States. As a result a few thousand shareholders organized and gained a great deal, while some 80 percent of the world's population lost significant access to patented medicines, for example.

Now, in this rule-shaping process, different powerful agents are differentially interested. In the TRIPS negotiations, the aforementioned four industries were very interested in intellectual property rights. However, banks may not care that much about intellectual property but do care deeply about the Basel rules. To achieve their ends, big and powerful players engage in horse-trading, which leads to a patchwork of heterogeneous and incoherent rules.

Still, there is an opportunity in all this. Big firms are caught in a prisoners' dilemma, and the wise option for big companies may be to constrain the influence of all big corporations because they have more to lose from other players' abilities to shape the rules in their own narrow interests than they have to gain from their own successful efforts.

Returning to your original questions, the counterproductiveness of the current system should be sufficient to prove that we *desperately* need a common moral basis, a common sense of fairness as a platform on which to build global governance. I think even the strongest players can be persuaded that this would be in their interest.

How do we organize such conversations?
TP: One possible track is forums like the World Economic Forum, which brings together several intelligent, far-sighted people who have already made their money and are looking for ways to do something positive and leave a legacy. I am optimistic about the possibility of engaging the Davos types.

But what you are doing, engaging the young people and giving them the tools to think about these issues intelligently, is very important and valuable as well. It is like reading five or six novels critically and with guidance at college, and becoming along the way an avid, thoughtful reader of literature for life.

You have talked about these issues in very different parts of the world. Are the reactions uniform or very diverse?
TP: You have all kinds of reactions—idealistic, cynical, skeptical, curious—in each classroom, especially if the class is large enough. You also almost always get a lot of shock in response to the extent and depth of poverty in the world. In contrast to the popular perception that in contemporary China everyone is only interested in getting ahead and making

money for themselves, I have found a lot of idealism there. Of course, there is also a strong tradition of respect for the teacher, and perhaps it is out of deference that I get these reactions; but I do not think this explains the whole picture. In the United States, there has been a trend of decreasing interest in issues of global justice. Interest has not disappeared entirely, but since the Reagan years, there has been an increasing prevalence of a "me first, U.S. first" attitude. With the end of the Bush era, the pendulum has started to swing the other way, but interest in global social justice issues is still far from the levels of the 1970s.

You have thought hard and written eloquently on issues of fairness. Does fairness matter?

TP: Realists argue that states are driven by their own interests and not by moral considerations. I am a realist of a different sort: if we cannot get a common moral basis established and ensure that it is effective, then we do not have much longer to go on this planet. My viewpoint is also realistic, but it is a different sort of realism: it is realism about what we need. So does fairness matter? It matters enormously. At the same time, fairness has to have substance, so that not everyone can claim it with a bit of rhetoric.

Are there thought experiments, works of literature or art that you have found useful in stimulating a thoughtful conversation about these issues?

TP: Literary works that vividly convey the conditions of life in other parts of the world are important. But there is not much available. This is not because this type of literature does not exist; there is a thriving literature out of Africa and India. But not enough of these works have been translated into English, and the ones that are in English are barely known. More people in the West need to encounter this literature.

Also, I would want to expose people to alternative data and analysis sources to counter the overly optimistic depictions of progress toward elimination of poverty and other ills. One-third of all deaths still occur due to poverty-related causes.

Finally, getting more people informed about the state of the world, and making sure that more or less comparable data are available to everyone may be the most important thing. It would be great if some parts of the global civics curriculum could be the same in all parts of the world. For example, we should be able to discuss what the fair way is to reduce greenhouse gases in commensurate ways in different parts of the world.

DANI RODRIK, *professor of international political economy,*
John F. Kennedy School of Government, Harvard University

I argue that current and future levels of interdependence necessitate a conversation about our responsibilities to noncompatriots and that a draft global civics should emerge. Would you agree or can we continue as is? Is there anything missing from our current menu of global governance?

DR: What is missing is a good sophisticated discussion on this subject. There is a literature from the ethicists and political philosophers on these questions. Peter Singer comes to mind, at one extreme. Amartya Sen has an important and nuanced position. On the other hand, we have people like John Rawls who attached a great deal of importance to national borders. As you know, Rawls does not think the veil of ignorance can be used globally. I firmly believe that this conversation needs to be taken out of the hands of the specialists and should permeate all classrooms. I teach a class on globalization, and a good deal of the content focuses on these issues. I personally grapple with these issues; I find myself closer to Rawls than to Singer.

Meaning borders matter?

DR: Borders do matter, but it is more important to distinguish between those areas where we truly have global responsibilities and norms, such as climate change and human rights, versus other areas. The innate value of someone in Rwanda is not less than the innate value of someone in the United States, and we all have at least a negative responsibility to not be a part of harming anyone one in Rwanda. In the case of climate change, it is beyond doubt that the atmosphere clearly constitutes a global public good, and whatever I do here that affects the atmosphere has as much effect halfway around the world as it does a mile down the road. However, we too often carry this mode of thinking into areas either where there are no global norms or where cross-border spillover is limited.

Economic development and the international regime of trade and finance are, comparatively speaking, examples of areas with limited cross-border spillovers and without obvious global norms.

But even to be able to make that distinction, don't we need to be cognizant of the effects of our actions on other people, even if they are noncompatriots?
DR: I see two different questions: What is the effect of my actions on others? And how much should I care about that effect?

Are there enough forums to deliberate either or both of these questions at Harvard?
DR: Although Harvard has always been a global university in a limited sense, it was significantly more insular ten years ago than it is today. Larry Summers, as president of Harvard from July 2001 to June 2006, had a lot to do with this change. Harvard did not have semester abroad or summer abroad programs until recently.

Yet something more than generic international exposure is needed, right?
DR: Absolutely. Presumably students need international exposure and experience precisely because they need to be a part of the global consciousness. The courses offered for incoming freshmen have become remarkably global. The ethos of globalization pervades to the extent that students may tend to assume that all areas, until proven otherwise, constitute a global public good. But maybe I perceive this because I do not teach the national security and foreign policy types.

We also know from the likes of the World Values Survey that most people are very attached to their national cultures. But national attachment does decrease with higher educational and skill levels.[4] So there seems to be something to this caricature of stateless elites who treat national borders as an impediment to the good life.

Do you have a favorite forum or modus operandi for these conversations?
DR: Too often we quickly dismiss views that differ from ours, and do not put ourselves in the shoes of other people. Yet, if we were to engage in a well-meaning and thorough conversation, we might well discover that we may have shortchanged the validity of their position. I find this to be

of critical importance. Greater online communication and interaction may be a remedy, since it has the potential to make us more tolerant and appreciative. This may be the key precursor to getting to global civics.

This process was observed in a Canadian town where some received comprehensive communication kits bringing the world to their feet.[5] There was also an unintentional control group, and at the end the people who had unhindered access to the world became much more neighborly and engaged with their community more effectively. In other words, global access and commitment need not happen at the expense of local attachments and commitments.

Does fairness matter?
DR: Fairness matters a whole lot. I think that reciprocity and fairness are hardwired into us. Research shows that people do accept a negative consequence if they view the process that brought it about as being fair. The legitimacy of global rules is a very significant part of their strength.

In the design of a course on global civics, what would you want to see discussed?
DR: I would put a lot of emphasis on trying to get the facts straight. What effect I actually have on others and what potential effect I can have are not easy questions to answer empirically. However, we cannot get to solid normative rules from faulty empirical bases or from wrong analysis of cause and effect. For example, Peter Singer's "drowning child" story is a very misleading analogy for the relationship between the developing and the developed world.[6] Too many times Peter Singer–type arguments underestimate what is needed to make a lasting difference and ensure that children do not face "drowning" again. On the other end, there is an alternative trap: cynicism and resignation over the extreme difficulty of making any difference in the lives of others. We need a lot of skepticism but no cynicism.

DINGLI SHEN, *professor of international relations and executive dean of the Institute of International Affairs, Fudan University, Shanghai*

Do we need a conversation about our responsibilities toward each other and about a global civics?

DS: I think global civics is a very timely and pertinent idea. We live in a global village. Shanghai to San Francisco is some ten hours by airplane and may someday take only two hours with new technology. Our proximity to each other is increasing daily. But the technologies that bring us together also have environmental consequences. We probably do not know the full extent of the damage our actions are causing. We need to be attentive to the already-known, as well as potential, consequences of our actions. And that requires a realization that people living in different countries share a common humanity, and a conversation about reasonable responsibilities we have toward each other. Despite of our different citizenships, we are also all citizens of the global village and have in fact much in common. I believe that most people are good and that we can agree on voluntary responsibilities toward each other.

So we need a social contract about how we are going to live in such close proximity in our global village?
DS: Yes, we do. It is like organizing traffic. Everyone has a need to drive, but if I drive in a manner that maximizes only my own interest, I create chaos and irrationality for others. Narrow individual rationality can end up as collective irrationality. This is why we need rules—our global governance regime—that maximize everyone's welfare.

Does fairness matter as we develop these rules and our global governance schemes?
DS: We always need morality, which has to do with conceptions of fairness. If some in the system consider the system to be very unfair, they may take destructive actions, such as terrorism. So fairness matters, but we should also not chase after absolute fairness, which is impractical and unhelpful. Furthermore, we need to balance competing claims of fairness; I would favor a rational fairness as a guide to our actions.

It has been argued that the philosophy of Kant in the West and the concept of ubuntu *in Africa or* vasudheva kutumbakam *in India provide us with useful benchmarks in the ethics of reciprocity and in thinking about our responsibilities to other residents of our planet. Are there similar tenets in the Chinese normative universe?*

DS: Well, Confucianism, our traditional philosophy, includes a strong belief in harmony between the people and the universe. Man cannot conquer the universe and should not hurt nature; according to Confucianism, humanity should operate harmoniously with its surroundings and the universe. Communism also gave us the language of human dignity and fairness. I believe we have the normative benchmarks and tools to talk about the ethics of reciprocity.

Should Fudan University or other Chinese universities include global civics in their curriculum?
DS: In the West man is thought to have committed the original sin. Therefore, we need civilization and the rule of law to correct the negative aspects of human nature. In China we traditionally believe that people are born with a benign nature. Nevertheless, people can be contaminated in a bad environment, so we believe that a good education and the positive influence of good surroundings can return people to their original benign state. In both paradigms a good education is beneficial. A liberal arts education at a university is the best method so far to bring out the most positive traits of human nature.

Our planet needs better international cooperation and better appreciation of our interconnectedness. Educated people have the primary responsibility in this regard. Universities have a responsibility and a mission to inform and enlighten the ordinary citizens. Universities are also the places where future leaders are trained. We need to do a better job in explaining our global problems and the need for international cooperation. I am optimistic for the long term, but the next ten to twenty years will be difficult, as there will be a big challenge to balanced development. This gives Fudan University even more importance in advancing the discourse of global civics.

Are your students interested in these issues?
DS: My students are definitely interested in global problems and in finding an appropriate role for China and for their generations in overcoming global problems. We are a leading Chinese university in teaching nonproliferation of weapons of mass destruction, where students have shown great enthusiasm in addressing the threats and overcoming them.

So, China taking a greater responsibility in solving our global problems can be a way to enhance China's soft power?
DS: China had experienced a curve of soft power. In the 1950s we championed the end of exploitation around the world. In the 1960s we supported Martin Luther King, and in the 1970s we supported the anti-apartheid movement. Since the 1980s we have become a more realistic actor, focusing on economic development and more cooperative on the world stage. With its recent success in the economy, China could further seek international acclaim by trying to help improve the international system, and taking increasing responsibility for solutions to global problems.

Should universities around the world cooperate in teaching global civics?
DS: You make a compelling case for a global civics education at universities around the world, and Chinese universities are in a position to make an important contribution to this effort. I think a global consortium of universities would be highly beneficial and meaningful. Fudan University would be happy to be a part of such a consortium. That consortium can be built around a shared philosophy, and different universities can have their own curriculum based on that shared philosophy and their national features, though we may need to be nuanced and sophisticated as we translate these notions to national and local frameworks. Fudan already has some partnerships, such as the one with Washington University in St. Louis on student effort concerning global zero of nuclear weapons. We can do even more on meaningful global civics education through enhanced international cooperation.

JAVIER SOLANA, *former minister of foreign affairs, Spain; former secretary general, NATO; and former high representative for common foreign and security policy, European Union*

Is our current menu of global governance schemes sufficient to manage our global interdependence?
JS: Profound changes are occurring in the world today including the megatrend of globalization. What we need is responsible interdependence—there is no other option. Interdependence is here to stay, and we have to

manage it in a responsible manner. Now, is the state the main unit of that responsibility? In the past the answer would have been yes. Today there are more actors than just the classical state, although the state continues to be the most important actor. We have gone much beyond the Westphalian order; the European Union is a good example. Now we have to go further and construct something like what you call global civics, via civil society and the Internet. It will not happen in a big bang. It will be a process and a very attractive, necessary, and timely one.

It will not be easy, simple, nor immediate. We have to understand different cultures, different religions, and different backgrounds. And a conversation, as you suggest, is the best way to get there.

In a way it should not be easy or immediate. We are in effect talking about a social contract—but this time a global one.
JS: Well, you know how many ups and downs and how much suffering were involved in getting to the national ones.

What would you tell the seven-billionth person, to be born a few years hence, regarding the life that awaits her?
JS: I am an optimist, so I will tell her about the good things. But I will also dwell on notions of responsibility and obligation that form the other side of opportunities and capabilities. She would need to be told that she is not alone and lives in varying proximity to many, many people, and that we are all interconnected. I will tell her about our predicament over responsible interdependence and ask her to advance this awareness because this will be key to her and her generation's welfare and survival.

There is also a school of thought that argues that interdependence does not matter but power does, and that all power is hard power. You have been at the top of Spanish, European, and Atlantic security and foreign policy for many years. Does this school of thought strike you as accurate?
JS: I think history and the world have proven these assertions wrong. So many of the problems we face today have no hard security solutions. I have actually been impressed by how widely it has been recognized that hard power is not the way that most of our problems can be solved today. It is easy to sound naive when talking about these issues, but I

do not believe I am being naive when I say that the shrinking world is pushing us together and that we can hammer out something like a global social contract.

Does Europe have something to offer to untangle this conundrum?
JS: Europe has several special characteristics, which I really love. Europe is the one place where a group of countries have decided, *freely and not by force*, to give up some of their sovereignty. Europe has realized a regional version of global civics, in a way. We are 500 million people, and within the European Union, we have the four freedoms: the free movement of people, goods, services, and capital. We do not pretend to teach anyone anything, but I suspect the European experience can be a source of inspiration for people around the world who are interested in these things.

Spain has been a beneficiary of the European solidarity and has been rather generous itself. Spain has refused to deny others the very same solidarity that helped Spain.
JS: I do not think it is just Spain. But if not all Spaniards, certainly the majority understands that we cannot deny others the dynamics that helped us to become free and prosperous. In general, I believe that the privileged have the responsibility to not only advance these ideas but also put them into practice.

What are the forums where you would look to see these issues being debated?
JS: I would look to the center of knowledge, namely, the university. Universities house people who should be by definition open to new ideas and global knowledge. We also have many global nongovernmental organizations that have done important work in generating pan-global consciousness and solidarity. And there is the Internet, which has created virtual citizens.

And broadcast TV, which has brought distress and bliss from faraway corners of the world to all living rooms?
JS: Sure.

Have there been works of literature, philosophy, arts, or theories of physics that have informed your understanding of how we are to manage our interdependence? Should a global civics curriculum include Cervantes or the unified theory of physics?

JS: You have not mentioned music! I do not want to lecture universities on what to include in their curriculum. I would think what one needs is an open mind. Any good book can be used to kick off a discussion of these pertinent issues. I have to say that I have a special concern for the experience of war and issues of peace, and Immanuel Kant impresses me in his treatment of these cardinal issues. I see him as an early global citizen or maybe an early advocate of a global civics.

Notes

1. Bill Bishop, *The Big Sort: Why the Clustering of Like-Minded America Is Tearing Us Apart* (Boston: Houghton Mifflin Harcourt, 2008).

2. Lynn Hunt, *Inventing Human Rights: A History* (New York: W. W. Norton, 2008).

3. Hakan Altinay, *Does Fairness Matter in Global Governance,* Global Working Paper No. 40 (Brookings, October 2010).

4. For more information about the World Values Survey, see www.worldvalues survey.org/wvs/articles/folder_published/article_base_51.

5. See Keith Hampton, "Netville: Community On and Offline in a Wired Suburb," in *The Cybercities Reader,* edited by Stephen Graham (London: Routledge, 2004), pp. 256–62.

6. See Peter Singer, "The Drowning Child and the Expanding Circle," *New Internationalist,* April, 1997.

THREE

Beyond the UN Charter:
A New Concept of Global Security
and Global Civics

NABIL FAHMY

Any student of global affairs will quickly come to realize that the international order within which we interact, and particularly the legal parameters that govern us therein, are remnants of the two world wars of the last century. In fact, the most prominent legal document of our time is without question the United Nations Charter, adopted soon after World War II. The legal foundation for our global order did not stop with, and is not solely based on, the establishment of the United Nations or the adoption of the UN Charter, which was preceded and followed by numerous international declarations and treaties such as the Universal Declaration of Human Rights, the Treaty on the Non-Proliferation of Nuclear Weapons, and recently the International Criminal Court. The present world order was also tailored by the political events over the last sixty years, which have generated numerous concepts and themes, such as the "global village," "globalization," and even "the clash of civilizations."

As international legal instruments and institutions developed over the years, there were continuous shifts in the global arena and a need for recalibration of some basic concepts, particularly as new stakeholders arose, including nonstate parties. The development of humanitarian norms and transparency associated with the communication revolution also brought into question singular principles of international law, such as the inviolability of states' sovereignty and noninterference in internal affairs of states. In the midst of all this, we have been torn between advocates arguing blindly in opposition to change, even though change was actually occurring, and those who believe that change *is* the objective and naively want to quickly discard much of what has held our world community together for so long.

Civics always involves a balancing act between rights and responsibilities. At the global level, the question that must be addressed before achieving a balance between the responsibilities of communities and those of individuals is, should we as states, nations, or individuals consider ourselves as the sum of our parts—highlighting and emphasizing, for example, the sovereignty of independent states—or as an integral whole with diverse traditions and experiences? To put it differently, is it more opportune to look at the world as an integral whole and try to make the best of our diversity rather than carrying it like an albatross that weighs heavily on our shoulders? I personally believe that both viewpoints can be found in the UN Charter. Therefore the challenge for global civics is to choose a basis, and at the same time advance both the letter and the spirit of the charter and the international norms that we have already established. Regrettably, contemporary international history is replete with evidence of states cherry-picking, emphasizing those concepts, norms, and interpretations of international legal instruments that serve their interests and ignoring others that highlight their responsibilities or the interests of others. Therefore, our optimism in this endeavor has to be tempered with caution.

The UN Charter provides ample evidence that the founders had the wisdom and foresight, even in the wake of the dramatic effects of World War II, to look well into the future and understand the importance of the documents they were developing. The preamble of the UN Charter starts with the words "we the peoples," a clear indication that the ultimate stakeholder is not the nation-state but the human beings that constitute each nation. On the other hand, the different articles of the charter talk about the responsibility and obligations of "states." This dichotomy was not an anomaly or meaningless coincidence, nor does it constitute an inadvertent contradiction, but it is a reflection of the delicate balance needed at that time to determine lofty and ambitious objectives while being pragmatic, realistic, and taking concrete steps forward.

Over half a century has elapsed since the UN Charter was adopted. Decolonization led to the expansion of the United Nations by over a hundred newly independent states. Other states have disappeared and some have reemerged. There has been an evolution of international organizations from the traditional intergovernmental model into other permutations that include both government and nongovernment representation, such as the International Labor Organization, and even into some more novel formats, such as the Internet Corporation for Assigned Names and Numbers (ICANN), which attempts to regulate the Internet. I mention these examples because they and many others encompass new sets of stakeholders and effective players in our global community and its institutions. These are the stakeholders in the new world order, and it is unwise to ignore the concerns and ambitions of this ever-expanding group.

As stated earlier, the present international norms were formulated essentially out of the vast losses, pain, and destruction of the two world wars of the last century, and consequently the global affairs paradigm was founded around an adversarial international system that tended to be security conscious and governed by what I now consider to be archaic political concepts and doctrines, such as "balance of power." Today two, if not three, generations of the global population have grown up in the post–World War II era. Their fears, challenges, and aspirations are of another world and were formed by a different set of experiences. And generations to come will find it even more difficult to relate to concepts from almost a century ago. In fact, for many youth even the cold war may soon seem medieval.

I do not suggest that we disregard the old world order or ignore the United Nations and its family of specialized agencies. Nor do I propose fundamentally changing the UN Charter immediately. What I do suggest is that we embrace a different concept of security based on "a balance of interests" rather than "a balance of power." This is much more commensurate and compatible with a world composed of multiple stakeholders, including both state and nonstate parties. There is really no other alternative.

At the outset the attempt to balance the interests of multiple stake-holders will be tedious and imperfect. It nevertheless would provide for a much more equitable outcome than the one we have today. Even more important, this more inclusive concept of balance of interests embodies not only the traditional definition of security, based on weapons, armaments, and sovereign borders, but also a more comprehensive set of parameters that have security and civic implications that account for economic and social interests—not only within and between states, but also among people across national borders.

To embed such new concepts and achieve these objectives will require courageous global leaders and principled statesmanship commensurate with that shown by the founders of the UN Charter more than sixty years ago. However, attempting to rapidly instill these concepts only through top-down state-to-state contacts will neither be successful nor productive because interstate competition, driven by short-term political expediency and the need to respond to the immediate aspirations of political constituencies, will work against long-term projects being imposed from above.

For these ideas to be highlighted and given enough exposure, they need to be adopted and promoted by political leaders who will address the importance of a new global vision founded on a larger concept of security. At the core would be a new social contract between the peoples of the world, one embracing the basic principle of "fulfilling the interests of different stakeholder[s] and maintaining a balance of interests." At the same time, unless there is a catastrophic event or circumstance that would unite the international community in support of a truly fundamental change in the international world order, a grassroots movement will be needed to advocate for the new paradigm. Academics, opinion makers, and social advocates are the natural leaders of such a movement, which can spread far more quickly than it would have in the past given the communications revolution and the extensive social networking of today. As these principles and concepts gain wider acceptance within our respective societies, they should lead to a more ambitious review of existing international mechanisms, with the goal of establishing more democratic governance globally, among all the states and not just within them.

In actuality, we have already engaged in a conversation about our responsibilities toward each other as residents of planet earth, as exemplified by the debates about sustainable development, poverty, environmental protection, and nuclear proliferation. What is missing is a conceptual framework to consolidate all this into a set of founding principles and governing parameters for the global community. One of the obstacles to having such a comprehensive discussion has been the fear that it would erode the UN Charter and leave us with less than what we have today—"the best being the enemy of the good," as the saying goes.

The natural place to plant the seeds of an all-inclusive conceptual structure would be in academia, particularly universities. It is always more effective to have discussions around a working document, or in this case, a "draft new security doctrine based on a novel social contract." However, I believe a more inclusive arrangement would be to listen to the different voices and opinions first while encouraging opinion makers, activists, and practitioners to address the topic at hand so as to encourage new ideas and not limit ourselves to defending or countering old arguments. This process can be initiated through a series of open discussions on relevant topics in the sanctuaries of academia, where freedom of thought is usually not shackled by overly structured or politically encumbered government policy.

Among the topics to be discussed would be:

—the definition of balance of interests;

—the scope and limitations of this concept as it applies to states—individually and as a group—and to societies and the individual, including the interests of the public versus the private sector;

—the intergovernmental organizational structure that would be required to oversee a world order based on such a concept; and

—whether or not a global parliamentary body can be established to at least deliberate, if not legislate, the legal norms that are required to govern such a system.

Such a series of discussions would be best served if they were to include practitioners from different disciplines, such as international security, economic and social development, and law. It would also be beneficial to engage some former practitioners, in order to bridge that ever important gap between vision and aspiration, on the one hand, and practical policymaking and governance, on the other. The results of these discussions would ultimately find their way into formal policy decisions, as has happened with the concept of global nuclear zero. These processes should lead to the publication of a comprehensive report or reports on the deliberations, and to sets of recommendations that would form the basis of a new global manifesto. The latter, drafted by a group of eminent individuals representing different walks of life, persuasions, and age brackets, would then be taken to higher governmental and parliamentary levels, both domestically and internationally.

Over the years, the middle power states—those outside NATO and the Warsaw Pact— have been strong proponents of an interdependent world and would welcome this exercise. The nonaligned countries, the Group of Seventy-Seven developing countries, and the members of the League of Arab States all fall into this category and would be natural supporters of the fundamental concepts of a balance of interests. Some of these states have gradually outgrown their traditional positions as their role in the international community has increased, and they are pursuing a more prominent place in the existing world order, even with all its inequities. Brazil and India are two examples as they strive for permanent membership on the UN Security Council.

Nevertheless, it would not be a stretch or unwarranted to suggest that middle power states would support a new focus on global civics in general and concepts like a balance of interests in particular. Celso Amorim, foreign minister of Brazil, has spoken often and written occasionally about the need for the international community to "listen to the other voices," a subtle though clear reference to the new emerging international players. Former UN secretary general Boutros Boutros-Ghali, who also served as Egypt's minister of state for foreign affairs for over a decade, had frequently advocated establishing a "more democratic" global system. Almost two decades ago, the late prime minister of India Rajiv Gandhi called for a nuclear-free world with equal rights for all states. The participation of King Abdullah of Saudi Arabia in gatherings such as the Group of Twenty reflects an increased activism by his country in issues that extend well beyond Saudi Arabia's geographical region. All these examples are indicative of a desire to be heard and engage in creating a global system that is more inclusive.

Support for global civics and a balance-of-interests doctrine exists throughout a diverse group of countries. However, the discussions about how to move these ideas forward at the grassroots level will vary, depending primarily on the level of education within given societies, the sophistication of their university systems, the strength of their nongovernmental organizations, and their system of governance. Most of these factors vary in sophistication across the Arab and Muslim world. Nevertheless, I believe that each and every one of these states already has a strong enough foundation to initiate discussions on these issues domestically and to participate at different levels in the global debates as well.

FOUR

Global Civics through Global Solidarity

TREVOR MANUEL and EDGAR PIETERSE

The core argument in "The Case for Global Civics" is that interdependence is a constitutive reality of the present global condition, in that almost all the major challenges facing humanity require a cooperative response that transcends the jurisdictional autonomy of nation-states.[1] This is not an argument to abolish the nation-state but rather a recognition that we need to strengthen and consolidate the nation-state in a much more explicitly interdependent global system, where new norms based on fundamental interdependence accelerate efforts to reregulate global economic and political affairs. Hakan Altinay regards this as particularly essential with regard to mitigating climate change and redefining the rules of international trade to achieve fairer economic distribution and opportunities. This intellectual project is fundamentally optimistic and rooted in a Habermasian confidence that through considered and structured "meritocratic dialogue," we have it within our powers as a species to confront our multiple and increasingly complex civilization crises.

The argument and tone of Altinay's global civics discourse stand in strong contrast to dystopian readings of the contemporary moment, as exemplified in the work of critical scholars such as Mike Davis. Davis suggests that the global political and economic society is simply not

Research support for this chapter was provided by Kim Gurney.

ready, interested, or equipped to confront the deep global crisis that is manifested in recent climate variability. In critiquing the emerging international discourse on climate change, he opines that:

> Of course, there would still be treaties, carbon credits, famine relief, humanitarian acrobatics, and perhaps the full-scale conversion of some European cities and small countries to alternative energy. But worldwide adaptation to climate change, which presupposes trillions of dollars of investment in the urban and rural infrastructures of poor and medium income countries, as well as the assisted migration of tens of millions of people from Africa and Asia, would necessarily command a revolution of almost mythic magnitude in the redistribution of income and power. Meanwhile we are speeding toward a fateful rendezvous around 2030, or even earlier, when the convergent impacts of climate change, peak oil, peak water, and an additional 1.5 billion people on the planet will produce negative synergies probably beyond our imagination.[2]

As South Africans perched at the southern tip of the poorest continent in the world—one whose people are frequently bombarded by all manner of crises beyond their making—we could be tempted to buy into Davis's fatalism. However, having also lived and struggled through the tyranny of apartheid (and its colonial precedents), we are also convinced that a more empowering vision and outcome are possible. This grows out of Manuel's direct involvement with the South African democratic experiment and with the efforts of the Growth Commission for Africa in recent years. This chapter seeks to work through the lessons of these exposures and to respond constructively to Altinay's invitation to flesh out the dimensions of a global civics in order to advance effective responses to the combined and intersecting challenges of population growth, inclusiveness, climate change, energy and water shortages, ecosystem degradation, and the related food crisis.

Imperative for a Global Civics and Solidarity

Altinay suggests that we should understand a global civics as "a system of conscious responsibilities which we are ready to take on after due

TABLE 4-1. Percent of People at Different Poverty Levels Worldwide, 2005

Units as indicated

Poverty line (dollars)	Population in poverty (in billions)	Population above poverty level (in billions)	Percent in poverty
1.00	0.88	5.58	13.6
1.25	1.40	5.06	21.7
1.45	1.72	4.74	26.6
2.00	2.60	3.86	40.2
2.50	3.14	3.32	48.6
10.00	5.15	1.31	79.7

Source: Shaohua Chen and Martin Ravallion, "The Developing World Is Poorer than We Thought, but No Less Successful in the Fight against Poverty," Policy Research Working Paper 4703 (Washington: World Bank, 2009).

deliberation and the corresponding rights that we are ready to claim"; this is a claim for ourselves and others because "doing unto others what we would have them do unto us remains the most resilient benchmark for decent conduct in human history."[3] Considering this framing, it is important to step back and take stock of what is being done to the vast majority of citizens in the global South, who live in low- and middle-income countries that are largely excluded, in democratic terms, from global rule-making—especially with regard to global economic relations that shape livelihood opportunities. In this context, we will briefly consider three issues: poverty levels, differential consumption capacities, and inequality.

Recent World Bank data indicate that based on an income poverty measure, almost 50 percent of the global population live on less than $2.50 a day. That is more than 3 billion people, almost all of whom are in developing countries (table 4-1).

Some people see this as progress. They argue that if one takes a historical view, it is clear that poverty is clearly trending downward. However, this kind of analysis tends to conflate the Chinese experience of the past three decades with that of all other developing countries. Table 4-2 clearly illustrates that if China is taken out of the equation, the ratio of people below the $2.50-a-day poverty line remains constant between

TABLE 4-2. World Poverty Levels, Including and Excluding China, 1981–2005

Units as indicated

Poverty line (dollars)	Number of poor people in the world (millions)								
	1981	1984	1987	1990	1993	1996	1999	2002	2005
1.00	1,515	1,334.7	1,227.2	1,286.7	1,237.9	1,111.9	1,145.6	1,066.6	876
1.25	1,896.2	1,808.2	1,720	1,813.4	1,794.9	1,656.2	1,696.2	1,603.1	1,376.7
1.45	2,137.7	2,111.5	2,051.7	2,153.5	2,165	2,048.1	2,095.7	1,997.9	1,751.7
2.00	2,535.1	2,615.4	2,639.7	2,755.9	2,821.4	2,802.1	2,872.1	2,795.7	2,561.5
2.50	2,731.6	2,858.7	2,944.6	3,071	3,176.7	3,231.4	3,316.6	3,270.6	3,084.7
	Number of poor people in the world excluding China (millions)								
1.00	784.5	786.2	814.9	787.6	793.4	823.2	843.2	821.9	769.9
1.25	1,061.1	1,088.3	1,134.3	1,130.2	1,162.3	1,213.4	1,249.5	1,240	1,169
1.45	1,244	1,293.2	1,348.9	1,365.3	1,418.9	1,488.1	1,541.7	15,43.5	1,535.2
2.00	1,563	1,652.1	1,732.7	1,795.1	1,895.2	2,009.9	2,101.9	2,140.8	2,087.9
2.50	1,759.5	1,895.4	2,037.6	2,110.2	2,250.4	2,439.2	2,546.4	2,615.6	2,611

Source: See Chen and Ravallion, "The Developing World Is Poorer," p. 41.

1981 and 2005. This is simply outrageous given the exponential growth in economic value and wealth that has been generated over this period as the globalization of the international economy intensified.

Another critical issue to keep in mind is that poverty is decreasing very slowly, and gains are not necessarily permanent. For example, in the wake of the recent global financial crisis, hundreds of millions of people sank back into poverty because of the absence of sufficiently robust safety nets. Based on this, we can anticipate that when income poverty data become available for 2009 and 2010, a number of these trend lines will be pointing upward again.[4]

It is beyond the scope of this chapter to explore the merits of the Chinese development path, given its unique hybridization of authoritarianism and economic liberalism premised on its market size and manufacturing dominance. Suffice it to say that it does not offer a realistic and resilient "model" for other developing countries to emulate in order to address the levels of widespread poverty referenced above—not least

TABLE   4-3. Distribution of the World's Private Consumption, 2005

Percent

Segment of global population	Share of private consumption
Richest 20 percent	76.6
Middle 60 percent	21.9
Poorest 20 percent	1.5

Source: World Bank Development Indicators, 2008, as cited at www.globalissues.org/article/26/poverty-facts-and-stats (September 2010).

because the energy intensity of the Chinese industrialization model is simply not sustainable from a resource consumption perspective.

On the subject of consumption, it is important to recast the poverty data with an understanding of differential consumption capacities. Tables 4-3 and 4-4 summarize inequality in consumption between those on opposite ends of the income spectrum.

Apart from the obvious moral and ethical problems associated with such extreme inequality of consumption, it is important to confront the implications of this in terms of mobilizing resources to address a number of fundamental human rights, as enshrined in the Universal Declaration of Human Rights. Some comparative expenditures shown in table 4-5 drive this point home.

Apart from the unacceptable prevalence of (income) poverty, we also know that it is being compounded by rising inequality. The troubling aspect of inequality is not merely the fact that it is getting worse but that there does not seem to be any moral bottom line for how much inequality is acceptable in a society, or globally for that matter.[5] In this regard South Africa is a difficult reminder of how much is required to address this condition in the contemporary global economic system. We will return to this theme shortly, but first we provide some data on the contemporary condition to demonstrate the scale of the redistribution challenge we are confronting. In 2006 the following disparities were observed:

—World gross domestic product (world population approximately 6.5 billion) in 2006 was $48.2 trillion.

—The world's wealthiest countries (approximately 1 billion people) accounted for $36.6 trillion dollars (76 percent).

TABLE 4-4. Inequality of Consumption, 2005

Units as indicated

World population by decile[a]	Percent of world's total consumption
1	0.5
2	1
3	1.4
4	1.9
5	2.4
6	3.3
7	4.8
8	8.1
9	17.6
10	59

Source: World Bank Development Indicators, 2008, as cited at www.globalissues.org/article/26/poverty-facts-and-stats (September 2010)..
a. World population decile: 1 = poorest 10 percent, 2 = poorest 11 to 20 percent, and so on.

—The world's billionaires—just 497 people (approximately 0.000008 percent of the world's population)—were worth $3.5 trillion.

—Low-income countries (2.4 billion people) accounted for just $1.6 trillion of GDP (3.3 percent).

—Middle-income countries (3 billion people) made up the rest of GDP at just over $10 trillion (20.7 percent).[6]

These alarming trends are evident as well in our own country, South Africa, and through a consideration of our challenges, we hope to illuminate the importance and value of the global civics imperative.

A South African Prism

The South African context is highly pertinent to the debates and issues raised by Altinay's invocation of a solidarity ethic under the rubric of a global civics rooted in a respect for everyone's human rights. The South African political liberation in 1994 arose out of a rather dark and seemingly intractable context. Reflecting briefly on the upsurge in state-sanctioned violence, we find it sobering to recall that the political violence between 1990 and 1994 led to 14,000 deaths and 22,000 injuries.[7] The death toll was much higher than at any single period during the

TABLE 4-5. Annual Spending versus Cost to Address Basic Needs, 1998

Billions of U.S. dollars

Consumption priority	Spending	Social development priorities	Cost
Cosmetics, United States	8	Basic education for all	6
Ice cream, Europe	11	Water and sanitation for all	9
Perfumes, European Union and United States	12	Reproductive health for all women	12
Pet foods, European Union and United States	17	Basic health and nutrition	13
Cigarettes, European Union	50		
Alcoholic drinks, European Union	105		
Narcotic drugs in the world	400		
Military spending in the world	780		

Source: Drawn from Anup Shah, "Poverty Facts and Stats," *Global Issues,* September 20, 2010 (www.global issues.org/article/26/poverty-facts-and-stats).

apartheid era.[8] Between 1984 and 1998, the highest number of deaths from political violence was recorded in 1993, when 3,794 people were killed, which illustrates just how serious the situation was on the eve of democracy.[9] This de facto condition of civil war placed severe constraints on the terms of the negotiated settlement that unlocked the agreement to pursue a democratic resolution to the intractable apartheid conflict.

Another set of constraints also presented itself. It is worth recalling that South Africa's political transition unfolded amid the economic globalization "revolution." Globalization presents very different faces, possibilities, and threats to different nations and organizations, depending on geography and history. As Manuel Castells continues to remind us, globalization generates various opportunities for growth and development in some places while at the same time profoundly marginalizing others. And perniciously, the more one is out of the "space of flows," as Castells refers to economic globalization, the more one is marginalized, and the less likely it is that one can generate the resources and networks to change that path-dependent condition.[10] Given the structure of the South African economy, its isolation after years of sanctions, and the need for large volumes of foreign investment, the government was compelled to come to terms with the "rules" of the global economic game and position itself to become an active member and advance its sovereign interests. All in all, South Africa found itself in a veritable macroeconomic policy pressure cooker that left it with very little more than vexatious options and decisions.

Despite the dual pressures of placating extremist white (racial) interests (who wielded financial power and firepower) while also entering a profoundly skewed global economy, we were still able to articulate and embed the core values of the South African liberation struggle through the enactment of one of the most radical and far-reaching (that is, "advanced") constitutions in the world. In reflecting on the human rights–based moral agenda that underpins Altinay's global civics, we find that it is consistent with the tenets of the South African constitution, which not only guarantees full political citizenship but also a commitment by the state and society at large to see the systematic realization of everyone's socioeconomic rights. Practically, this means a commitment to the right to freedom of movement, safety, environmental protection, housing, health, and economic opportunity. This commitment has created a strong imperative to keep public policy and discourse focused on how well the state, in conjunction with civil society and the private sector, is doing in realizing these rights. Now, asserting a rights agenda does not automatically mean it comes to pass, as will be explained below. However, the key challenge is to, at least, have the normative base in place while navigating the demands of a plethora of complex and intractable vested interests, some of which often are beyond the formal control of the state. We are certain that there is a lesson in this approach for the broader debate on what a global civics may mean in our highly unequal and divisive world. But first we will briefly clarify the scale and scope of the South African development challenge, which incidentally mirrors the larger condition of global apartheid as set out in the earlier part of this chapter.

As is to be expected after more than forty years of apartheid racial engineering, which was based on a profound colonial legacy, South Africa's black population is deeply impoverished. South Africa does not have a single official poverty line, so various studies calculate income poverty in different ways. Even though debates remain strident among poverty

TABLE 4-6. Narrow and Broad Measures of Unemployment in South Africa, 2001–09[a]

Percent

Measure	2001	2002	2003	2004	2005	2006	2007	2008	2009
Narrow	25.4	27.2	27.1	23.3	22.6	22.3	23.5	22.9	24.0
Broad	33.1	35.0	35.9	34.6	33.2	31.8	32.3	27.5	30.1

Source: Organization for Economic Cooperation and Development, *OECD Economic Surveys: South Africa 2010* (Paris: OECD, 2010).

a. The narrow definition excludes discouraged work seekers, defined as people who have not looked for work during the fourteen days before the survey was conducted.

experts, there is broad agreement that between 1993 and 2000, poverty declined only marginally, whereas after 2000, with a significant rise in employment and the dramatic increase in social grants, it fell. For our purpose, it is instructive to cite the findings of Murray Leibrandt and his colleagues, who found that there were 18.5 million poor South Africans in 2000 and a decrease to 15.4 million in 2004.[11] Eighteen million people represented almost half of the South African population in 2000. One of the key drivers of large-scale and structural poverty in South Africa is unemployment. Despite the country's middle-income status, a very large proportion of the labor force cannot access formal employment, as shown in table 4-6.

The apartheid legacy, combined with deindustrialization and inadequate educational outcomes for poor people, translates into very severe income inequality in South Africa. With a Gini index of 0.7, South Africa has one of the worst levels of inequality in the world, though a substantial and rising social wage, in the form of free schooling, water, housing, electricity, and health care for the poor, has contributed to improved living standards.

In a society with such severe development problems, it is self-evident that the rights agenda of the constitution can only be realized through a gradually rising floor and a sensible redistribution program. The South African government has been able to develop and continuously refine one of the most substantive social development programs in the global South. The key elements of the national social security package, targeting poor individuals and households, are set out in box 4-1.

BOX 4-1. Social Security and Other Redistributive Instruments in South Africa

South Africa does not have comprehensive social security for the unemployed, but in 2009 it did provide a number of similar benefits, as shown below:

Grant	Number of beneficiaries
State old age pension	2,343,995
Disability grant	1,371,712
Child support grant	8,765,354
Foster care grant	476,394
Care dependency grant	107,065
War veterans grant	1,599
Total	13,066,119

In addition to these social security grants, the government has an extensive program to facilitate access to basic services for the poor. To implement this each municipality is required to have an indigents' register in order to administer the following subsidies:

—Free basic water: 6 kL (6,000 L) per month per household.

—Free electricity: 50 kWh per month per household for a grid energy system.

—Free sanitation: 100 percent of rate (charge) if household income is below a certain level.

—Housing subsidies: since 1994 more than 2.3 million housing units have been made available for nearly 11 million people. The value of these subsidies has in recent years increased after it failed to keep pace with inflation between 1996 and 2002. The subsidy translates into a transfer of a serviced house and title to the beneficiaries. Due to the cost of the program, there remains a considerable waiting list, but on average approximately 300,000 of these subsidies are disbursed per year.

—Transport subsidies: made available for people who use the bus and rail public transport modes.

Source: Adél Bosch and others, "A Second Look at Measuring Inequality in South Africa: The Gini Co-efficient Revisited," unpublished paper (Pretoria: Reserve Bank of South Africa, 2010).

These investments have enabled South Africa to simultaneously pursue a growth agenda while mitigating the worst intergenerational effects of long-term social injustice against black people. However, given the country's slow progress toward reducing poverty and inequality, it is clearly not enough. There are a number of deep structural dynamics at play that we are now in the midst of coming to terms with and confronting. For example, it is extremely difficult to deal effectively with the crisis of structural unemployment because our educational system is experiencing a deep institutional crisis that arises from the confluence of poorly trained teachers, weak school-level management and leadership, undercapitalized infrastructure, and inappropriate curriculum reform, all of which by definition have been difficult to change once the big policy shifts were effected after 1994. This is in addition to the problematic social conditions—crime-ridden neighborhoods and dysfunctional families—within which most of our schools operate. It is clear that as long as we are unable to achieve much better outcomes for our educational investments (which are already among the highest per capita in the global South), we will be unlikely to solve our unemployment crisis. As time passes it becomes increasingly difficult to break this vicious cycle because the scenario fosters a multigenerational problem of compounded exclusion and its associated social pathologies, such as familial violence, drug abuse, social conflict, and the deterioration of mutual support systems. This social patterning in turn becomes a compound dynamic that disproportionately affects the youth from poorer backgrounds. As a result the demographic youth bulge turns what should be an economic dividend into a profound social and spiritual cost and crisis.

The work of the Commission for Africa captured a very similar dynamic at work in the rest of Africa as the majority of the continent's states are coming into robust economic growth: although national wealth is increasing, it only accrues to a small middle-class elite, and the vast majority of the population gets left even further behind in terms of prospects for accessing formal and decent jobs. In fact, eight out of every ten entrants into the labor market in sub-Saharan Africa work at an informal job, reflecting a global trend toward informalization.[12] Thus it is now estimated that the informal sector accounts for up to 70 percent of all nonagricultural jobs, a situation that is entwined with the fact that 60 percent of urban Africans outside of South Africa live in informal dwellings.[13] This structural informality means that the state is unlikely to derive sufficient revenues to invest in the massive infrastructure that is needed to foster more inclusive and sustainable forms of growth in Africa.[14] On the contrary, whatever investments are available—especially from new sources in Asia—are restricted to the production of a spatial economic form that reinforces Africa's role as a supplier of raw materials into the manufacturing and industrial hubs of other countries and continents. If new forms of financing for labor-intensive infrastructure development and maintenance are not identified and implemented soon, it is difficult to see how Africa's marginal position in the global economy will change or where the resources will come from to address the continent's vast socioeconomic and environmental needs. Since much of the current situation can be traced back in various ways to centuries of misrule and exploitation, it seems obvious that the concept of global civics could open up important new areas of debate about how global solidarity can translate into investment resources to address the African condition. Of course, it goes without saying that such a debate must be predicated on clean and democratic governance and rooted in a deep respect for the law and the autonomy of civil society.

Toward Global Governance Reform

If the current patterns of economic development and need persist into the twenty-first century, or if reductions in poverty proceed as glacially as during the 1981–2005 period, it is clear that the normative ideal underpinning global civics will remain a cruel mirage. However, it is important to recognize that the most important obstacle to a fairer world, one open to new forms of negotiated solidarity and mutuality, is the lack of institutional transformation of global governance systems in the domains of politics, economics, and the environment. The outdated and obsolete institutional architecture that we have inherited from the post–World War II era has been roundly critiqued and reconceptualized for at least the past three decades.[15] Yet reform has remained painfully elusive. Well-reasoned and -argued alternatives have largely fallen on deaf ears despite consistent proposals from states in the developing world, global civil society organizations, and high-profile philanthropists such as Bob Geldof and George Soros. However, this is all seemingly about the shift.

For example, during the Copenhagen climate change summit in December 2009, President Obama found himself outnumbered when he attended a hastily convened final hours meeting with the Chinese prime minister Wen Jiabao. *The Economist* reported that "when the president turned up, he found not only Mr. Wen but the heads of government of Brazil, South Africa and India. This was unexpected. . . . What was conceived as a bilateral talk turned instead into a negotiation with an emerging-market bloc."[16] This new reality is reflected in turn by the elevation of the Group of Twenty (G-20). It seems inevitable that the Group of Seven will no longer be able to determine global policy as emerging markets have an increasing impact on the global political economy. This is clearly the view of leading global governance expert David Held, a professor at the London School of Economics, who writes that the financial crisis resulted in the emergence of the G-20 as the new de facto governance coalition of powerful states, reflecting "the new changing balance of power in the world." Whereas the old threat was "the other," Held says that the new threat consists of shared, collective problems: "To sum up, realism is dead, long live cosmopolitanism."[17]

This new geopolitical configuration stems from the fact that developing countries are increasingly sources of global liquidity, having huge foreign reserves and a direct interest in changing the rules of the global financial game. This involves, inter alia, the use of an alternate reserve currency and, most notably, voice and vote reform of the international financial institutions, particularly greater representation in the Bretton Woods institutions.[18]

The issue of reforming the Bretton Woods institutions has come into much greater relief thanks to the Zedillo report on World Bank reforms and the Manuel Commission report on International Monetary Fund (IMF) reforms, both published in 2009.[19] The latter included recommendations to create a council of ministers and governors with rotational representation, revise quota allotments to allow a greater voice for developing countries according to their economic weight, and promote a merit-based selection process for managing directors.[20] The Manuel-chaired report states that "the IMF's advice has lost traction and effectiveness in recent years, reflecting drawbacks in its governance structure on several fronts, including inadequate voice and representation and hence ownership of emerging markets and developing countries."[21] Apart from improving the representativity of the World Bank and IMF, it is equally important to pay attention to the Financial Stability Board (formerly the Financial Stability Forum), which extends beyond the Group of Seven to include G-20 regulators). Although it stands to be the most important international financial regulator, its board is "narrowly and arbitrarily construed" and excludes most developing countries, according to Arjun Jayadev, professor of economics at the University of Massachusetts.[22]

Given the need for global governance reform, South Africa and its partners in Africa have been keen to explore informal interim mechanisms to enhance the voice and footprint of our excluded continent. The upshot has been the creation of the Committee of Ten African Ministers of Finance and Central Bank Governors, which supports South Africa in its preparations for participation in the G-20 processes.[23] Although informal and ad hoc, the Committee of Ten helps formulate and coordinate African positions for international meetings and develops protocols that manifest the openness and flexibility that will be required to lead by example as institutional reform gains momentum.

It is of course critical to remain aware that the reregulation and democratization of the global financial system is but one dimension of many pressing issues facing the international community. As Jayadev underscores, growth of global inequality, the energy and food crises, climate change, global pandemics, and other such challenges are equally urgent; and in the face of such upheavals, the nation-state has lost some of its "viability" as the primary site for dealing with these changes.[24] This point is of course central to Altinay's insistence on the need to find a new set of agreements and reference points for regulating global affairs, given that all of these issues are so profoundly interdependent and intertwined.

Thus it would be a serious error to think that these imperatives can be left in the hands of states to fulfill. As David Held reminds us, states now find themselves embedded in much more complicated sets of social and political relationships, leading to a world of multilayered power and authority and to increasingly complex forms of governance. "A shift is taking place from states as simple 'containers of political power' to states as just one layer, albeit an important layer, in a complex political process in which state sovereignty is a 'bargaining chip' for use in negotiations over extensive transnational phenomena."[25] Held further suggests that three sets of problems need to be confronted as we redefine the scale and scope of global regulation: sharing our planet (global biodiversity and ecosystem losses, water deficits), sustaining our humanity (conflict prevention, controlling global infectious diseases), and revising our rulebook (regarding nuclear proliferation, toxic waste disposal, intellectual property rights, genetic research rules, trade rules, and finance and tax rules).[26] The resolution of all these problems requires collaborative action, reinforcing the basic premise of greater interdependency embedded in the idea of a global civics.

The Politics of Global Civics

"In an increasingly interdependent world, we need a corresponding global framework to put our minds at relative ease. Part of that reference framework has to be based on global civics, a system of conscious responsibilities which we are ready to take on after due *deliberation* and the corresponding rights that we are ready to claim."[27]

In reflecting on this assertion by Hakan Altinay, we want to conclude with a brief reflection on the idea of consensus versus contestation. At the heart of Altinay's approach to forging a new agenda for a more inclusive and humane world is the deep belief that through rational deliberation we can arrive at a series of compacts or agreements on the terms of a global civics. Here we part ways with his Habermasian confidence in the power of rational deliberation and lean more closely toward the democratic philosopher Chantal Mouffe, who insists that robust agonistic conflict is an essential prerequisite for transformative change.[28] In his interpretation of Mouffe, Edgar Pieterse explains that "we can never fully reconcile the tensions between equality (maximization of egalitarian spaces of differences) and liberty (maximization of democratic rights), but instead deploy the tension to animate agonistic contestation within the ambit of universal human rights. . . . The tension produces agonistic pluralism in the polity," whether it be at the neighborhood, settlement, national, or global level.[29] The agonistic tension is a vital energizer for hard-nosed democratic debate and is crucial for contestation about competing policy agendas and world views. Unless we can connect some of the fundamental questions of our age to their foundational elements, we are unlikely to get to the root causes of global incivility.

Global civics, as important as it may be, cannot be a substitute for the efforts of elected representatives to whom the people have given clear and unambigious mandates. In conclusion, the huge utilitarian value of a well-organized and interconnected global civics movement must balance responsibility and voice with the views of legitimately elected representatives. Only through such balance can we derive the maximum benefits of a global civics.

Notes

1. Hakan Altinay, "The Case for Global Civics," Global Economy and Development Working Paper 38 (Brookings, 2010).

2. Mike Davis, "Who Will Build the Ark?" *New Left Review* 61 (January-February 2010): 29–46, 38.

3. Altinay, "The Case for Global Civics," pp. 4 and 6. See also chapter 1 in this volume.

4. See International Monetary Fund and International Labor Organization, "The Challenges of Growth, Employment and Social Cohesion," Joint conference, Oslo, 2010.

5. Duncan Green, *From Poverty to Power. How Active Citizens and States Can Change the World* (Oxford and Johannesburg: Oxfam International and Jacana Media, 2009).

6. Drawn from Anup Shah, "Poverty Facts and Stats," *Global Issues,* September 20, 2010 (www.globalissues.org/article/26/poverty-facts-and-stats).

7. It is noteworthy that "between 1948 and 1999, an estimated 13,000 people were killed in the Israeli-Palestinian conflict." See Patrick Neate and Damian Platt, *Culture Is Our Weapon* (London: Latin American Bureau, 2006), p. 102.

8. Oscar A. Barbarin and Linda M. Richter, *Mandela's Children: Growing Up in Post-Apartheid South Africa* (London: Routledge, 2001) p. 76.

9. Mirjam van Donk and Edgar Pieterse, "Contextual Snapshots: Development Challenges and Responses during the Transition," in *Voices of the Transition. The Politics, Poetics and Practices of Development in South Africa,* edited

by Edgar Pieterse and Frank Meintjies (Johannesburg: Heinemann Publishers, 2004), pp. 38–52.

10. Manuel Castells and Martin Ince, *Conversations with Manuel Castells* (Cambridge: Polity, 2003).

11. For a comprehensive account of the poverty debates and numbers, see the authoritative report by Murray Leibrandt and others, "Trends in South African Income Distribution and Poverty since the Fall of Apartheid," Social, Employment and Migration Working Paper 101 (Paris: OECD, 2010), p. 18.

12. UN Human Settlements Program (UN-HABITAT), *State of the World's Cities 2010/2011: Bridging the Urban Divide* (London: Earthscan, 2010) p. xiv.

13. Ibid.

14. These investments were recently quantified as $50 billion a year, on top of the current levels of $45 billion to begin to address the massive infrastructure requirements of sub-Saharan Africa. See Vivien Foster and Cecilia Briceño-Garmendia, eds., *Africa's Infrastructure: A Time for Transformation* (Washington: World Bank, 2010).

15. See Commission on Global Governance, *Our Global Neighbourhood* (Oxford University Press, 2005).

16. "The Trillion-Dollar Club," *The Economist,* April 15, 2010 (www.economist.com/node/15912964?story_id=15912964).

17. David Held, "The Changing Face of Global Governance: Between Past Strategic Failure and Future Economic Constraints," *Social Europe Journal* 4, no. 1 (2010) (www.social-europe.eu/2010/01/the-changing-face-of-global-governance-between-past-strategic-failure-and-future-economic-constraints/ [September 2010]).

18. That is, the World Bank and the International Monetary Fund.

19. Ernesto Zedillo, *Repowering the World Bank for the 21st Century: Report of the High-Level Commission on Modernization of World Bank Group Governance* (New York: United Nations, 2009). See also Trevor Manuel and others, *Final Report of the Committee of Eminent Persons on IMF Governance Reform,* 2009 (www.imf.org/external/np/sec/pr/2009/pr0988.htm [September 2010]).

20. Arjun Jayadev, "Global Governance and Human Development: Promoting Democratic Accountability and Institutional Experimentation," Human Development Research Paper (New York: United Nations Development Program, 2010).

21. Manuel and others, *Final Report.*

22. Jayadev, "Global Governance and Human Development," p. 24.

23. Daniel Bradlow, "The Global Financial Architecture: Is Change Coming?" *Global Dialogue: An International Affairs Review* 14, no. 1 (2009): 16–18.

24. Jayadev, "Global Governance and Human Development," p. 5.

25. Montserrat Guibernau, "Globalization, Cosmopolitanism and Democracy," interview with David Held, March 11, 2001 (http://politybooks.com/global/globalization-cosmopolitanism-and-democracy.asp [September 2010]).

26. Held, "Changing Face of Global Governance."

27. Altinay, "The Case for Global Civics," p. 4, emphasis added. See also chapter 1 in this volume.

28. Chantal Mouffe, *The Democratic Paradox* (London and New York: Verso, 2000).

29. Edgar Pieterse, "The Limits of Possibility: Working Notes on a Relational Model of Urban Politics," in *Urban Africa: Changing Contours of Survival in the City,* edited by Abdou Maliq Simone and Abdelghani Abouhani (Dakar: Codesria Books, 2005), p. 163.

FIVE

Civic Involvement
at a Turkish University

TARA HOPKINS and TOSUN TERZIOĞLU

M any people from various walks of life, in different countries or regions, discuss globalization, meaning the various manifestations of the integration of national or regional economics through a globe-spanning network of communications and trade. While the exact definition of globalization may be argued, few would deny such a process exists. We are all affected somehow by what others do elsewhere, not only by direct investments, outsourcing, and the behavior of stock markets but also through human migration, trafficking of persons, and even fashion trends and the accessibility of certain soft drinks or coffees. This incomplete list is certain to become longer as we go forward, since globalization is an ongoing, complex process.

Eric Hobsbawm notes in *The Age of Extremes—The Short Twentieth Century* that the "most striking characteristic of the end of the twentieth century is the tension between this accelerating process of globalization and the inability of both public institutions and the collective behavior of human beings to come to terms with it."[1] Apart from the usual national public institutions, there are those that are international or supranational, such as the United Nations, European Union, the North American Free Trade Area, World Trade Organization, International Monetary Fund, World Bank, and the International Criminal Court, to name just a few from an ever-growing list. In dealing with global issues, however, the efforts of such agencies may be obstructed by some nations. Here are just two examples.

Founded in 2002, the International Criminal Court is a permanent tribunal to prosecute individuals for genocide, crimes against humanity, war crimes, and crimes of aggression. It was only recently—June 2010—that the definition of aggression was agreed upon, and this is with the stipulation that the International Criminal Court would be able to exercise jurisdiction over such crimes, "but only over those committed one year after 30 States Parties have ratified the newly-made amendment."[2]

In the last two decades, several world-renowned economists and even some prominent members of the U.S. legislature have proposed bold schemes such as a global tax on carbon emissions and currency trading, and a global resources dividend. Many of the proponents hoped that the UN would be the natural forum for debates on various financing schemes for global public goods, but all these proposals were ultimately blocked by unilateralists and sovereignists in powerful countries.

The concept of a "global civics"—one that could serve to make us all more responsible and responsive residents of the planet that we share—is insufficiently discussed or even understood. People have protested against oppression, climate change, the "haves" over the "have nots," and many other global problems. Though protesting can be regarded as an attempt to voice an idea and stand for change, it does not entail taking much responsibility for the outcome. What our age lacks is the notion of responsibility, individual or collective, for global issues and problems—in short, a true global civic involvement.

The residents of our planet are citizens of different nations. Each nation-state has its own flag, national anthem, laws, armed forces, taxes, and history. Some nations, more than the others, carry a heavy burden of traditions, ideologies, and fear—or sometimes even hatred—of "the other," and these act as deeply rooted obstacles to change. Each nation has a specific policy for education, and one of the priorities of such a policy, at least in primary education, is to ensure that the future generation is raised to become loyal and obedient citizens of the nation-state. Civics has to do with citizenship, referring to educating the citizens of a nation within a given political and ethical framework. However, a global civics should address people as citizens of our planet and help them to understand and be responsive to global issues and problems, which are far beyond the reach of national policies and sometimes are in conflict with short-term national interests.

Many trends point to our apparent interconnectedness. The number of international tourist arrivals reached 1 billion in the recent years, up from a mere 70 million in 1960. The number of Internet users exceeded 1 billion in 2005, and soon it will exceed 2 billion. Over 3 billion of us are mobile phone subscribers, talking with people living in other continents, getting news, sending messages, and enjoying banking services, all while sipping tea or coffee in a cafe. As residents of our planet, we are certainly connected, yet our minds are not! When that finally happens, we will no longer be only residents but also citizens of the world.

Except under the most repressive regimes, there are many possibilities for and benefits from implementing programs for civic education in university systems everywhere. Universities are perfect venues for young people, who often are both idealistic as well as critical and have extra energy. They need to learn more about the inner workings of their own society, to study the more complicated aspects of human history as a whole, and to see themselves as citizens who have rights and responsibilities that go much deeper than a purported birthright.

We would like to share our own story about how, at Sabanci University, we had the rare opportunity to design a program for direct participation by all undergraduates: the Civic Involvement Projects (CIP) program. Sabanci University is a private university, established in 1999; though situated in Istanbul, it considers itself a world university. The CIP program is one of the distinguishing features of the university, along with a highly interdisciplinary approach and a total commitment to academic freedom.

It was agreed from the beginning that the program should be part of the curriculum and a graduation requirement. There were various reasons behind this decision. First, those working at the venues where the students would be assigned needed to be convinced that the time and energy required to collaborate would be justified because they would actually benefit from student involvement. Because of previous experiences or preconceived notions or suspicions, civil society organizations and state-run institutions may harbor doubts about students' motives as well as dedication. Making the program part of a curriculum does not erase all suspicions but does help minimize them. Such an arrangement also fosters greater communication between the university and the local community, as there will be numerous opportunities not merely to meet face-to-face but to genuinely cooperate.

We wanted the CIP program to be an integral part of the school's foundations program, where all undergraduates progress through a two-tier common curriculum in their freshman and sophomore years before they declare their majors. A two-semester freshman course in the foundations program called Humanity and Society is particularly relevant to any civics education. Combining elements of social and economic anthropology with the history of political thought, this course first focuses on kinship-based society, tributary states, and early commercial civilizations. The second semester is wholly devoted to the emergence, successive agendas, dynamism, and tortuous byways of modernity, in both its Western and non-Western forms. Humanity and Society ultimately converges with another course, Science of Nature, and concludes with an examination of possible agendas for the twenty-first century in the context of globalization.

The CIP program runs for an academic year, with an average project participation time of two to three hours a week. As part of the curriculum, the program tries to encompass a wide variety of topics to expand its appeal to a variety of students. Generally students contribute and learn more if they work on an issue for which they feel some affinity. In actuality, however, program topics are limited by the venues with which we can partner, which by default forces the students to think globally yet act locally. Many civil society organizations in Turkey operate with professional staff and have little use for volunteers; many that do use volunteers require more expertise and life experience than our (mostly) eighteen-year-old freshmen have. About half the projects are conducted with state-run organizations in cooperation with the Ministries of National Education and of Social Services and Children's Welfare.

An essential aspect of our CIP program is student training. This is implemented at the most basic level and covers the importance of teamwork, creative problem solving, and, perhaps most important, learning to look at one's work through the eyes of those who run the respective organization. Drawing upon the educational philosophies of John

Dewey and Lev Vygotsky, the program was designed and operates on the premise that students learn by doing and that they create their own knowledge. The role of the educators is to facilitate this process. Within the Turkish context, we must acknowledge that to get to this point, the program initially had to be more top-down than we would have wanted. Nevertheless, such structure was congruent with our own argument that we could not expect students to understand what was expected of them if they had never had exposure to direct civic involvement.

Once the program was under way, it was a natural next step to involve students in positions of responsibility. From the beginning the projects were carried out in teams, but in the second year, students became team leaders. This first group of students worked closely with the coordinator, meeting weekly to discuss progress, frustrations, challenges, and highlights, and to work on building the team. We were inventing a structure that eventually would be replicated throughout the program, one based on teamwork, weekly meetings, and learning to allow for different ideas and opinions while fostering a deep belief in what we were doing: teaching others and ourselves to make a difference through direct involvement from the bottom up. Though we were in effect forcing our students to "give a damn," we established a framework that mirrored what we wanted students to learn. While we acknowledged that they did not *yet* have the skills they needed, we committed ourselves to providing the guidance *and* then trusted the students to apply it. Surprisingly, we have had a good turnout of students who committed themselves to volunteer for the CIP program in successive years, even though their curricular obligations were done.

The CIP program is not without its flaws, and we are constantly making changes as we continue to grow, learn, and incorporate new ideas from different players. It is not easy to measure the success of such a program, and it certainly would not be easy or credible to do so from within our own structure. However, we can look at various indicators. While we were the first university to establish such a program in Turkey, there are now twenty universities throughout the country with similar projects. While we do not expect our students to go on to professional careers in civil society, we are proud that a number have done so, largely due to the impact of their experience in the CIP program. It is also important to note that some graduates who are pursuing a totally different professional life have also incorporated civic participation into their careers.

We were fortunate to have the backing of the university's board of trustees and the administration to establish our program. We plowed ahead because we could. At many international conferences, we received accolades and requests for assistance to help start up similar programs, even in Western countries.

For such a program to be effective, it is important to work within the current system, speak the local language as it were, and earn the trust of those entities whose collaboration is needed. One must remember that the very nature of such a program implies a criticism of the current status quo—and that can be threatening. One must make the program's goals clear, not only to students and faculty but also to those who will serve as vehicles for this learning. The latter especially must be involved in the process from the beginning and must be made to feel that they have an essential role to play, which they do. In the enthusiasm of trying to implement change, it can be easy to dismiss the background of those you are working with to try to implement those very changes. That cannot be allowed to happen. Hence extra care and patience are needed to communicate in a manner that is respectful and understood by all players.

It is also essential to offer as wide a range of topics as possible for students, so that even the most reluctant participants will find an area where they can fit in. A student who engages with an issue that may be close to his or her heart or outlook on life will gain and offer exponentially more than if the work is not in an area of interest.

For our own part, we know that we would have benefited tremendously if we had been connected with other institutions in other parts of the world that were pursuing similar goals. Although we are idealists, we are also human. The challenges of this kind of program are great and can be tiring. Thus a supportive network is essential to stay on the path to positive change, to not only encourage but lead the way for young people to become more aware of the impact of their actions on their local as well as global environment. Teaching others how to make a difference is an inseparable component of the democratic process, and it needs to be a part of university curricula everywhere. And to achieve this end, we first need a network of like-minded institutions around the world. Global civics is an essential building block to the sustainability and well-being of the planet. Let's get to work.

Notes

1. Eric J. Hobsbawm, *The Age of Extremes: The Short Twentieth Century, 1914–1991* (London: Michael Joseph, 1994), p.15.

2. UN News Center, "After Years of Debate, ICC Member States Agree on Definition of Aggression," June 14, 2010 (www.un.org/apps/news/story.asp?NewsID=35018&Cr=&Cr1=).

PART II

Developing a Global
Civics Curriculum

SIX

Discussing Global Civics

HAKAN ALTINAY

A discussion of global civics need not entail a fourteen-week semester format or even a formal classroom setting. Students can come together in an extracurricular setting under some facilitation and explore the issue through an agreed upon reading list. Adults who are not in an academic environment may engage in a similar pursuit with their peers.

Below is my outline for a set of miniworkshops for that purpose.[1] The outline is designed to be modular. One does not need to cover all of the issues and each suggested workshop, although if a critical mass of content is not there, the exercise may become hollow. Furthermore, a series of conversations on global civics is necessarily a multidisciplinary and multimedia affair. Therefore, not only scholarly works but documentaries, websites, and literary works should be included in the curriculum. Dividing up the material for each workshop among the participants and asking some to lead the presentation and discussion of each work can be a method conducive to the interaction needed in this exercise.

Workshop 1: The World We Live In

Any attempt to start to think about a global civics needs to commence with establishing a baseline and a balance sheet about the world we live in. The United Nations and the World Bank have extensive data that are available online for anyone's perusal. Penguin Group USA publishes a *State of the World Atlas* series, which presents some of those data in a visually comfortable format.[2] In the same vein there is also *The Global Citizen's Handbook*.[3] Websites such as gapminder.org allow for interactive inquiries.

The World Values Survey (www.worldvaluessurvey.org) and World Public Opinion (www.worldpublicopinion.org) can provide answers on what people in different parts of the world think on a wide range of issues. The World Values Survey has the added advantage of having completed five rounds, which allows one to track over time critical changes, such as support for gender equality across the globe. It also has a user-friendly interface that allows nonspecialists to analyze its vast database with remarkable ease.

Contextualizing where we are also requires us to grasp where we have been. There are too many histories of the world to choose from here. Each group can identify a couple for themselves. However, omitting Angus Maddison's work on the broad historical trends in the world economy would be a significant loss.[4] Westerners have an understandable tendency to assume that their own reality—likely to be urban and modern—is the dominant lifestyle. However, we need to be reminded—and to remember throughout our pursuits—that other realities exist. Ron Fricke's film *Baraka* (1993) should be a part of all global civics viewing lists; it is a remarkable visual presentation of human diversity and would serve as a helpful challenge to default assumptions. Similarly, Richard Nisbett's book *The Geography of Thought* is a powerful reminder that formidable intellectual traditions and cognitive frameworks outside the Western tradition exist and need to be taken very seriously.[5]

Workshop 2: Centripetal Forces—Globalization and More

As we start to conceptualize where we stand, all those centripetal forces pushing us together deserve a review. *Globalization* is the catchall term for what has been happening, and there is a rich literature to draw from: *The World Is Flat* by Thomas Friedman, *In Defense of Globalization* by Jagdish Bhagwati, *Globalization and Its Discontents* by Joseph Stiglitz, and *Manifesto for a New World Order* by George Monbiot are a few diverse works by popular journalists and academics to make sense of the multiple changes taking place and what we should think about them.[6]

The standard literature on globalization draws heavily from economics and political science, and yet there is an inevitable story of technological change that should be told and appreciated. I find Sidney Pike's *We Changed the World* and Nicholas Negroponte's *Being Digital* very valuable, not least because both of them had front row seats to the two recent and highly consequential transformations that we have come to take for granted.[7] Yet, if you think satellite television and the digital revolution explain everything, then you have to read Marc Levinson's *The Box* to be reminded what an astonishing difference the standardization and proliferation of shipping containers have made.[8]

There is one more work that I want to suggest: *A Movable Feast: Ten Millennia of Food Globalization* by Kenneth Kiple.[9] This book is not only a delight to read and provides a refreshing perspective about something as ubiquitous as food, but more important, it is a powerful reminder that human interaction across long distances has been happening for much longer than the past thirty years. Nayan Chanda's *Bound Together* is a similar work on early manifestations of globalization.[10]

Workshop 3: Climate Change

Nothing drives home our epic global interdependence more than the climate. Thanks to a recent increase in interest in this issue, there is a rich menu of literature from which to choose. My favorite is the documentary *The 11th Hour* (2007), directed by Leila Conners Petersen and Nadia Conners, and produced and narrated by Leonardo DiCaprio. *The 11th Hour* is a thoughtful discussion about the environment, with the participation of a diverse group of experts, including Lester Brown, Nathan Gardels, Mikhail Gorbachev, James Hansen, Steven Hawking, Wangari Maathai, David Suzuki, and James Woolsey.

The website of the International Panel on Climate Change (www.ipcc. ch) is a worthwhile resource. A very useful web-based tool is the Climate Analysis Indicators Tool, created by the World Resources Institute (cait.wri.org). It provides critical information on things like the historical emission of greenhouse gases by various countries. Organizations such as 350.org (www.350.org) and Contraction and Convergence (gci.org.uk) also provide useful alternatives in thinking about solutions.

Workshop 4: Genocide

Since World War II it has been recognized that genocide is the ultimate crime and that we all have a responsibility to stop it. And yet this seemingly simple principle rarely seems applied in real life. Thinking through what it means to face a genocide and what our responsibilities are is central to a global civics.

For those with enough time, Claude Lanzmann's documentary *Shoah* (1985) is a must. Its exceptional length, more than nine hours, should not be allowed to deter viewing. We need something more than *Schindler's List* (1993) to begin to appreciate the gravity of the Holocaust. Reading Philip Gourevitch's powerful book about the Rwandan genocide, *We Wish to Inform You That Tomorrow We Will Be Killed with Our Families*, and watching the documentary film *Shake Hands with the Devil* (available in a fifty-two-minute classroom edition) are also a must.[11]

Despair is a natural response when taking a close look at the extraordinary evil that is possible, and thus we need a discussion of what recourse we have. *The Reckoning: The Battle for the International Court* (2009) is a documentary that depicts the work of International Criminal Court prosecutor Luis Moreno Ocampo and provides viewers with a glimpse of this new institution. *The Responsibility to Protect* by Gareth Evans chronicles the development of a new norm and is highly informative.[12] I suggest that this session also include Gary Bass's *Freedom's Battle*; humanitarian intervention does have a problematic history, and we owe it to ourselves and everyone else to know and grapple with that legacy.[13]

While not an idea with imminent prospects of being realized, the proposal for a United Nations Emergency Peace Service to Prevent Genocide and Crimes against Humanity is nevertheless worth debating, if for no other reason than to understand what the impediments are to such an obvious solution to this grave problem.[14]

Workshop 5: Poverty, Development, and Trade

It is not difficult to become desensitized to constant streams of data about human misery from around the world. Therefore if we are serious about really examining the issue of poverty, I suggest using less obvious material and reading instead *Never Let Me Go* by Kazuo Ishiguro and *Respect* by Richard Sennett.[15] Neither is easy reading, but the issue is a grave one and merits something more than dismissive and fleeting attention.

As we start to come to terms with poverty and disenfranchisement, we would want to think about what can be done. The Millennium Development Goals are one tool the world has, and Jeffrey Sachs has been involved closely with their evolution. His book *The End of Poverty* will provide readers with solid insight into the mode of thinking behind this approach.[16] *Global Crises, Global Solutions*, edited by Bjorn Lomborg, has all the charm and limitations of a contrarian position.[17] Not everyone has to like the findings presented, but the research methodology is difficult to disagree with. It is a must-read for anyone interested in making a difference in the world.

Finally, despite so many years of debate, international trade still is an unsure sell. I find Russell Roberts's *The Choice* pedagogically very attractive without being overly simplistic, and feel that any review of these issues would be lacking without it.[18]

Workshop 6: Risks

Which of these is a bigger risk for an average human being: a nuclear bomb, an AK-47, a land mine, or malaria? To prepare for this workshop, the participants would read the Nuclear Non-Proliferation Treaty and study the websites of various initiatives including Global Zero (www. globalzero.org), the International Action Network on Small Arms (www. iansa.org), the International Campaign to Ban Landmines (www.icbl. org), and the Drugs for Neglected Diseases Initiative (www.dndi.org). They would then assess what the impartial positions on all these risks should be and compare those positions with the actual positions of various national governments and other stakeholders.

Workshop 7: Global Governance

Having unbundled several fields, we can circle back and think systematically about how to manage global problems in need of global solutions without a world government and through the voluntary cooperation of many diverse governments and ever more diverse nonstate actors.

Paul Kennedy's *The Parliament of Man* and Strobe Talbott's *The Great Experiment* provide us with much thought and information as a basis.[19] *A Better Globalization* by Kemal Derviş shuttles between the ideal and the feasible without doing injustice to either.[20] *Global Public Goods* presents a coherent paradigm for considering one option for global governance.[21] If one needs an alternative view, *The Return of History and the End of Dreams* by Robert Kagan attempts to persuade us why we should not have any faith in these lofty ideas.[22] In the same vein, the Global Governance Watch website (www.globalgovernancewatch.org), a program of the American Enterprise Institute and the Federalist Society, provides a number of arguments why we should be wary of global governance.

Workshop 8: Values in an Interdependent World

As the review of various global governance options would reveal, we need to talk about the values underlying our institutions before we can decide which institutional constellation is desirable. *One World* by Peter Singer and *Power Rules* by Leslie Gelb provide diametrically opposed views on values in the context of global interdependence; Singer advocates a radical cosmopolitanism, whereas Gelb sees no use for such a philosophy.[23] Gelb does not pose the only opposition to Singer's perspective; *Cosmopolitanism* by Kwame Appiah makes an eloquent and nuanced case in favor of a differentiated ethics for an interdependent world, and is a must-read in this context.[24] Another valuable perspective is provided by Jeremy Rifkin in his book *The Empathic Civilization,* in which he undertakes the ambitious task of reconfiguring major chunks of social science and humanities while arguing for the creation of an empathic civilization, not only as a normative imperative but as a model necessitated by the laws of energy.[25]

Another approach to global values that merits exploration is that of the Catholic theologian Hans Küng, who has advocated for a global ethics since the early 1990s. In collaboration with the Council for a Parliament of the World's Religions, he drafted the Declaration toward a Global Ethic.[26] A complementary and worthwhile exercise might be to research and debate *ubuntu, vasudheva kutumbakam,* and the golden rule.

Finally, we need some way to engage and address the cynicism that permeates popular culture and everyday life. From popular self-help books to the TV show *Seinfeld*, we are repeatedly told that life is not fair and it is silly to lament the obvious. And yet manifestations of kindness and generosity with no expectation of reciprocity seem to have a resilient presence. There are two movies, *The Lives of Others* (2006) and *Pay It Forward* (2000), that may help us ponder these issues. Both have a thoughtful and endearing story line, and redefine what is possible in terms of choices facing all of us. As such they merit a prominent place in this curriculum.

Workshop 9: Global Civics 2.0

In this final workshop, participants would be asked to come up with their own answers to two of three assignments:

—What would you tell the seven-billionth person, who will soon join us on Earth, about the life and the world that awaits her?

—If you were the speechwriter of the next UN secretary general, what would you have the secretary general say at the next UN General Assembly?

—If you were asked to address the World Economic Forum plenary in Davos, what would you tell the attendees?

The group would then discuss each submission and assess whether there are compelling similarities or differences. In case of significant overlap, the group can compile individual submissions along with their version of Global Civics 2.0 to be shared with other peers.

Notes

1. Nihat Berker and I are running such a workshop series at Sabanci University in Istanbul throughout 2010–11.

2. See Dan Smith, *The Penguin State of the World Atlas,* 8th ed. (New York: Penguin, 2008).

3. World Bank, *The Global Citizen's Handbook: Facing Our World's Crises and Challenges* (New York: HarperCollins, 2007).

4. Angus Maddison, *The World Economy* (Paris: OECD Publishing, 2006).

5. Richard E. Nisbett, *The Geography of Thought: How Asians and Westerners Think Differently . . . and Why* (New York: Free Press, 2003).

6. Thomas Friedman, *The World Is Flat: A Brief History of the Twenty-First Century* (New York: Farrar, Straus and Giroux, 2005), and subsequent editions; Jagdish Bhagwati, *In Defense of Globalization* (Oxford University Press, 2004); Joseph Stiglitz, *Globalization and Its Discontents* (New York: W.W. Norton, 2002); George Monbiot, *Manifesto for A New World Order* (New York: New Press, 2004).

7. Sidney Pike, *We Changed the World* (St. Paul: Paragon House, 2005); Nicholas Negroponte, *Being Digital* (New York: Knopf, 1996).

8. Marc Levinson, *The Box* (Princeton University Press, 2006).

9. Kenneth Kiple, *A Movable Feast: Ten Millennia of Food Globalization* (Cambridge University Press, 2007).

10. Nayan Chanda, *Bound Together* (Yale University Press, 2007).

11. Philip Gourevitch, *We Wish to Inform You That Tomorrow We Will Be Killed with Our Families: Stories from Rwanda* (New York: Farrar, Straus and Giroux, 1998).

12. Gareth Evans, *The Responsibility to Protect* (Brookings, 2008).

13. Gary J. Bass, *Freedom's Battle: The Origins of Humanitarian Intervention* (New York: Knopf, 2008).

14. See Robert C. Johansen, ed., *A United Nations Emergency Peace Service to Prevent Genocide and Crimes against Humanity* (New York: World Federalist Movement–Institute for Global Policy, 2006). Also available at the website of the International Coalition for the Responsibility to Protect (www.responsibilityto protect.org/files/UNEPS_PUBLICATION.pdf).

15. Kazuo Ishiguro, *Never Let Me Go* (New York: Vintage Books, 2006); Richard Sennett, *Respect* (New York: W.W. Norton, 2003).

16. Jeffrey Sachs, *The End of Poverty* (New York: Penguin, 2006).

17. Bjorn Lomborg, *Global Crises, Global Solutions* (Cambridge University Press, 2004).

18. Russell Roberts, *The Choice* (New Jersey: Pearson, 2007).

19. Paul Kennedy, *The Parliament of Man* (New York: Random House, 2006); Strobe Talbott, *The Great Experiment* (New York: Simon and Schuster, 2008).

20. Kemal Derviş, *A Better Globalization* (Washington: Center for Global Development, 2005).

21. Inge Kaul, Isabelle Grunberg, and Marc Stern, eds., *Global Public Goods: International Cooperation in the 21st Century* (New York: Oxford University Press, 1999).

22. Robert Kagan, *The Return of History and the End of Dreams* (New York: Knopf, 2008).

23. Peter Singer, *One World* (Yale University Press, 2002); Leslie Gelb, *Power Rules* (New York: HarperCollins, 2009).

24. Kwame Anthony Appiah, *Cosmopolitanism: Ethics in a World of Strangers* (New York: W.W. Norton, 2006).

25. Jeremy Rifkin, *The Empathic Civilization* (New York: Penguin, 2009).

26. Hans Küng and the Council for a Parliament of the World's Religions, "Declaration toward a Global Ethic," presented and signed at the Parliament of the World's Religions, Chicago, September 4, 1993 (www.weltethos.org/dat-english/03-declaration.htm).

SEVEN

Global Civics through Literature

MURAT BELGE

The concept of "global civics" means a lot to me because I have
always believed that the content of "civics" can never be fully realized unless it is at the same time "global." Consequently, I am delighted
to have been asked to write about literature as a way of conceptualizing
global civics and incorporating recommended reading.

At the outset I should state that all art, all good literature, contributes
to a global civics without necessarily aiming to do so. Art and literature
enrich the human consciousness—and conscience, too—and strengthen
the common bonds of humanity. Therefore I did not search for novels
that are explicitly concerned with civics issues. There certainly are such
novels, and many good ones among them, but those that address such
issues in a more oblique way can be more powerful, precisely because
they are concerned with the general and not strictly specific cases.

I have limited myself to the novel, and further, mostly to the novels
of the twentieth century. As I have already mentioned, I do think that all
art is relevant for this framework and that the novel tradition from Cervantes to Dostoyevsky is extremely rich in consciousness-raising of any
kind. However, I prefer to limit myself to the twentieth century because
the problems dealt with in these novels are necessarily contemporary and
more familiar.

There is one nineteenth-century novel, however, that is in many ways a potent metaphor for our age: Mary Shelley's *Frankenstein*. We all know the almost droll way this piece of literature came into being: the Shelleys, with their friends Lord Byron and his doctor, J. W. Polidor, were having a vacation at Villa Diodati near Lake Geneva in 1816. Staying in because of the constant rain, they passed the time by reading or talking about ghost stories and horror tales, until Byron suggested each one of them to try his or her hand at a supernatural story. Mary Shelley started her work as a short story but could not restrain herself or her "story."

The subtitle of this novel is "The Modern Prometheus," Prometheus being the mythical figure who defied the gods by giving fire to mankind. Between him and Dr. Frankenstein is, of course, the character Faust, immortalized by Goethe but borrowed by him from many medieval folktales as well as from Marlowe's play. In a nutshell, *Frankenstein* is the story of intellect gone mad, as well as of intellectual arrogance, the insatiable yearning for knowledge, and the creature turning against the creator, all of which are meaningful in our age of nuclear weapons, destruction of nature, violent ideologies, and harmful side effects from advanced technology. We can judge the potency of this novel, written half in sport, by the numerous movies that it directly or indirectly inspired.

I start my reading list with the classic twentieth-century dystopian work, *1984* by George Orwell. Many readers of this most widely read book feel happy that its prophecies have not come true. The world is not shared by three powers, and dictatorships of the kind drawn in this novel have not been established. But when we think of those ubiquitous and suffocating aspects of our contemporary life that are not so visible because they have already become ordinary, the picture does not look so bright. What is really important in this context is not so much the institutional structure of dictatorship as its impact on the individual, and this is brilliantly depicted in *1984*, especially the end, where betrayal and emptiness turn to love for one's tormentor and oppressor.

It is probably due to the dialectics of life that a notion of global civics becomes possible as the result of a study of the very factors that impede or stifle it. In this vein I would recommend Joseph Conrad's *Heart of Darkness*, a work that precedes *1984* by nearly half a century. But its potent symbolism can affect us in any era, just as it affected Francis Ford

Coppola in the context of his 1979 Vietnam War film, *Apocalypse Now*. "The horror! The horror!" mutters Mr. Kurtz at the end of his strange life. Unfortunately, this is a very apt word to describe so many experiences of our age. The novel is an excellent study of the potency of dark forces, and of the aspirations and dangers of the human psyche.

1984 was inspired by the dictatorial regimes of the thirties and the forties, and by Stalinism in particular. The failure of socialism, which to so many intellectuals carried the promise of universal liberation, was a serious blow, causing deep disappointment. One of these intellectuals was Arthur Koestler, whose *Darkness at Noon* I add to my reading list. In contrast to what I said about the advantages of a book of general import, this one does address a very specific and concrete case, that of the Stalinist purges of the thirties. The hero, Rubashov, bears a strong resemblance to Nikolai Bukharin, a key figure in the Russian Revolution. The strength of these old Bolsheviks' reverence for the Party and their sense of sacrifice are powerfully drawn. Koestler also points to the important differences between the generations and between the liberating universal intellectual, Rubashov, and the liberated masses, as personified by the diabolical manager of the prison.

From Koestler I take a short step to John Steinbeck and his novel *In Dubious Battle*. In his relationship with socialism, Steinbeck did not undergo as drastic a change as Koestler did, but then his commitment had not been as deep—he was more of a fellow traveler rather than a comrade. *In Dubious Battle* is a bitter book, perhaps even more so than *The Grapes of Wrath* (his epic about the Okies). It tells us a lot about political struggle, working class organization, and state repression. But my preference for including this novel in the list is the ending, which indeed is very dubious. Of the two socialist protagonists, one dies, and the novel ends as his comrade makes an agitated speech, using the other's corpse to strengthen his argument. There is no author evaluation of this outcome, but I take his lack of comment as a question posed to us, the readers: What are the limits of politics and ethics? Can everything be turned into an instrument for the cause? These questions are still quite cogent.

The next suggested reading is William Golding's *Lord of the Flies*. As Mary Shelley's *Frankenstein* contains references to Prometheus and Faust, this novel refers to and acts a polemic against all previous Robinsonades.

Among others, the philosopher Jean-Jacques Rousseau was influenced by Daniel Defoe's 1719 novel *Robinson Crusoe,* in particular, the basis for his noble savage, that mythical figure who keeps his human purity because he is not contaminated by civilization. But more than Defoe's work, Golding targets R. M. Ballantyne's *Coral Island,* with its depiction of shipwrecked English boys setting up an idyllic society. Golding defies not only the notion of nature as inherently good but also of children as inherently good. Some of the children in his novel are good because they have been educated to be sociable, but the worshipers of the Lord of the Flies, the other group that develops in a fascist way, exhibit the collective evil and urge for destruction, in certain ways reminiscent of the horror of Kurtz. To the sailors who ultimately rescue the children without knowing anything about the tragedy that took place on the island, these are just ordinary boys, and yet they have been capable of so much cruelty. This contradiction is a powerful—and wordless—comment on the human predicament.

The Tin Drum is the most important story of Günter Grass's Danzig Trilogy. It is a strange and unique blend of realism and fantasy, and those parts of the story that transpire in Danzig are the ones most firmly impressed into the readers' minds. As a picaresque novel, *The Tin Drum* has the advantage of presenting a panoramic view of a society or a part of the world and is inhabited by many people of various kinds. The actions of this motley crowd are highly fantastic and symbolic as well as full of mystery. Why does the protagonist Oskar not grow, and what does that signify? That he can shatter glass with his voice is evocative of the Kristallnacht, but is he anti-Nazi or partly a Nazi himself? The difficulty of giving precise answers to such questions increases the impact of the book rather than creating an atmosphere of ambiguity that leads nowhere, a phenomenon typical of much recent postmodernist fiction.

Stephen Dedalus, like his creator James Joyce, refused to serve Irish nationalism. During the first quarter of the twentieth century when Irish nationalism was rife, in the arts as well as politics, an Irish writer was expected to write in Gaelic, which Joyce refused to do. No one can say that *A Portrait of the Artist as a Young Man* is a political novel. Yet it is replete with Irish politics, like anything else that Joyce wrote. The paradox is that everywhere in the world, one is bound to come across at least one Irish pub, and the majority of these pubs are called "The James Joyce Pub"! Is it not amazing that this writer who not only defied Irish nationalism—though writing about almost exclusively on Irish topics—but also exiled himself from Ireland should universally become the symbol of Irishness? This fact demonstrates the power of art. Joyce's adamant *non serviam* provides a different but very valuable example of global civics. The narration of the "young artist's" struggles with sin, the church, and Catholicism is also a terrific psychological study.

Another trilogy I felt obligated to include in this reading list is *Into Their Labours* by John Berger. In the first two volumes of the trilogy, *Pig Earth* and *Once in Europa,* Berger deals with the disappearance of peasantry in the world. Modern technology and capitalism have rendered the peasant class obsolete. This way of life is fast disappearing, and the author wants to understand it before this happens. Since understanding can come only through shared experience, John Berger decided to live in a mountain village in Haute-Savoie to work with the peasants and learn their ways. He still spends part of his time in this village.

In his third volume, *Lilac and Flag,* Berger examines the issue of immigrant workers, who were mostly peasants in their own countries and became workers in the host country. Here, apart from the age-old class distinctions, there is the additional factor of being foreign. Migration and internal populations of foreigners are two burning issues of the contemporary world in need of a global civics approach.

A much older novelistic study of the encounter between two very different cultures, which can turn into a clash because of the depth of the difference, is E. M. Forster's *A Passage to India.* In this highly sensitive novel, a young English woman has a strange experience in a mystic cave and tries to make her experience understandable to herself by accusing a Muslim Indian doctor of sexually molesting her. The haughtiness of the colonizer culture is inevitably the most significant component of her behavior, though the writer tries to avoid stereotyping the white European's racialism. It is not so much individuals as their cultures that create these barriers and lead to such misconceptions, misunderstandings, and miscommunication. What the native suffers under the weight of this false accusation is less the focus here than the discomfort of the "superior" race.

Desertion is a novel by Abdulrazak Gurnah, a writer from Zanzibar living in Britain. It also addresses cultural gaps and interracial issues. Several years ago Fredric Jameson, a Marxist literary critic and political theorist, started a debate by claiming that all, or almost all, works of narrative fiction produced by third world authors are political or national allegories. This is probably the result of certain writers employing this literary method to give an account of the history and peculiarities of their country. If *Desertion* can be classified as an allegory, it is a very subtle one indeed. There are two story lines. The first follows the Englishman Martin Pearce, who appears near Mombasa, half dead, and is brought back to life and recovers by the efforts of the natives, notably Hassanali. He then falls in love with Hassanali's sister, Rehana, only to abandon her to return to Europe after the brief romance. In the second part, we meet Rehana's granddaughter and her generation about half a century later. Here, too, is a case of desertion, this time by a man of the same nationality. If this is an allegory, I interpret it as a statement that although there is the inevitable superior-versus-inferior dichotomy in the general imperialist situation, this dynamic continues even after power is nationalized.

The Golden Notebook by Doris Lessing can also be partly classified as picaresque though the work challenges the traditional structure of the novel. It was published in 1962, still some years before the vigorous feminism that arose in the late 1960s. *The Golden Notebook* cannot be labeled as a feminist novel, but it expresses a feminine sensibility and meaningfully touches upon so many areas that became issues of heated debate or struggle in the various feminist movements. Lessing obviously has her own sense of civic responsibility as well as an internationalist grasp of the world.

I want to include William Faulkner's *Light in August* because it is a brilliant study of some of the possible ways that racialism in the United States could develop. Faulkner, like Joyce, is not a political writer, and his temperament is not at all like that of Orwell, Koestler, or Conrad. He limited himself to the world he knew best, thus writing almost exclusively about the South; yet, paradoxically, he was able to universalize his themes in this physically and historically narrow context. Though Faulkner did not have a political tendency, politics could not absent itself from the various levels of his depictions of life in the South, the Civil War, slavery, and abolition. The mode of existence in this social context provides the subject matter of most of his novels, but in *Light in August,* the racist mentality and puritanical evangelical upbringing of certain white characters play out in a starkly frightful reality. Not only those who have chosen to hate blacks but also those who profess a certain liking for them are irreparably crippled by the dominant racialist ideology.

Another work that I have in mind is *The Trial* by Kafka, though it could be *The Castle* as well. How shall I define Kafka's novels? Allegory? Fantasy? Their dreamlike atmosphere does not tell us much about a specific society or any specific, concrete time and space. His setting is always much more unreal than Faulkner's fictional Yoknapatawpha County. It can only exist in Kafka's imagination, even if some claim that the castle must be the palace—the Prazsky Hrad—above the Mala Strana (Lesser Quarter) section of Prague. Perhaps it is, but Kafka's world is always abstracted several levels beyond the real world.

What, then, has Kafka to tell us about global civics? Well, a lot, really. The angst in his works, which immediately pervades our minds as well, may be caused by anything. But the cause is not so important. What matters more is the omnipresent, subjective feeling of guilt in Kafka's anonymous protagonists, the feeling that somehow their absurd predicament is deserved. And yet the moral sensibility of his protagonists is not nullified by the nightmarish situations in which they find themselves. Despite the intensity of the angst, Kafka never invites us to total surrender.

My final choice is *Never Let Me Go* by Kazuo Ishiguro. His earlier novel, *Remains of the Day,* was a masterful study of class distinction and class ideology; however, I believe the later novel makes a greater contribution to any consciousness of global civics because it is an incredibly subtle study and a damning condemnation of exploitation. The world in *Never Let Me Go* is a dystopia that has arisen after a third world war. Humankind has developed a technology for breeding human clones, who are allowed a brief life so that they ultimately can give their organs to first-class human beings. It is one of the saddest novels ever written, in the usual calm manner of Ishiguro, with the unbearable pain of what is not spoken. Selfishness—that probably endless human capacity to justify anything that is useful for the self—and the extraordinary ability to "otherize" the victim are the main themes of this book, and as such, are of utmost value in any discussion of global civics.

The fact that I have chosen two dystopias in a list of fifteen works is, I think, interesting in itself and should not be explained by personal leaning. I could easily have included Aldous Huxley's dystopias, *Brave New World* or *Ape and Essence,* or similar works by many other fine writers, such as Yevgeny Zamyatin. It just seems that this genre suited the general atmosphere of the twentieth century. If cultivated thoughtfully, a global civics may change this for the twenty-first century.

EIGHT

A Global Civics Syllabus for 2011–12: Introduction to Concepts and Theories

GRAHAM FINLAY and VUSI GUMEDE

This chapter proposes and assumes the form of a sample syllabus for a fourteen-week course in global civics, roughly as it would appear in a course catalogue, with content summaries and assigned reading and viewing. Global civics is concerned with questions regarding the rights and responsibilities of human beings toward each other in an increasingly interconnected and interdependent world. In chapter 1 of this volume, Hakan Altinay describes global civics as "a system of conscious responsibilities that we [humanity] are ready to assume after due deliberation and corresponding rights that we are ready to claim." These rights and responsibilities are not necessarily attached to each person's membership in a particular state or to particular international institutions. They are compatible, in most cases, with the rights and obligations one has to one's country and do not require a world state. In some cases, however, they have come to be expressed through international agreements and agencies, as explored in this course.

Crucial to global civics is a particular understanding of rights and responsibilities. The British sociologist T. H. Marshall described the evolution of rights in Western societies from "civil" rights (rights to certain treatment before the law) to "political" rights (rights to participate in one's society) to "social" rights (rights to certain social protections).[1] International human rights practice speaks of three "generations" of rights: civil and political, economic and social, and collectively held rights, such as the right to self-determination or development. This syllabus covers, for the most part, the first two generations, although collective solutions to international problems such as climate change have sometimes been addressed in terms of collective rights. But regardless of what rights are under discussion, if these rights are simply thought to be entitlements that someone is passively granted or can enjoy without responsibilities, then the "civic" aspect of global civics is lost. Only when these rights are viewed as essentially related to a person's active engagement with his or her world—as something that individuals can claim as a participant in a community and, accordingly, as something that imposes responsibilities on them—do they constitute dimensions of global civics.

In the various materials below, we consider the interdependencies, common spaces, and institutions that unite people across borders and the implications of these for our common humanity. We then look at Marshall's three types of rights and emphasize the ways in which they express the agency, views, and choices of the individual people who hold them and the responsibilities they impose on other people. Although global civics is compatible with a variety of institutional forms, it is nevertheless essentially concerned with justice. In its understanding of justice, our module concludes with the seminal but different works of John Rawls and Amartya Sen. Through Rawls we are led to the question of a hypothetical global social contract. From Sen we adopt his vision of "rights as agency" and "development as freedom."

The syllabus is geared toward three principal learning outcomes. The student will

—develop a good understanding of the interplay between national, local, and global justice;

—acquire a good understanding of the core principles underpinning the call for global civics; and

—appreciate the pros and cons of global civics.

Week 1: Introduction

During the first week, students are introduced to the idea of global civics. We will discuss the possibilities of democratic deliberation in the international context and gather students' expectations about the possibilities of global civics. Using Kwame Appiah's article, we will consider the global aspects of the lives of different people, rich and poor, and ask how these interdependencies contribute to global awareness. We also briefly consider the role of a "theory" of justice, based on the work of John Rawls.

Readings

Hakan Altinay, "The Case for Global Civics," Global Economy and Development Working Paper 38 (Brookings, 2010).

Kwame Anthony Appiah, "The Case for Contamination," *New York Times,* January 1, 2006 (www.nytimes.com/2006/01/01/magazine/01cosmopolitan.html).

Nigel Dower and John Williams, eds., *Global Citizenship: A Critical Introduction* (New York: Routledge, 2002).

Archon Fung, "Deliberation before the Revolution: Toward an Ethics of Deliberative Democracy in an Unjust World," *Political Theory* 33, no. 3 (2005): 397–419.

Zenobia Ismail and Paul Graham, "Citizens of the World? Africans, Media and Telecommunications," Afrobarometer Briefing Paper 69, May 2009 (www.afrobarometer.org/abbriefing.html).

Steven Kull, "Listening to the Voice of Humanity," *Kosmos*, Spring-Summer (2010): 26–29 (www.kosmosjournal.org/kjo2/backissue/s2010/index.shtml).

John Rawls, *A Theory of Justice* (Harvard University Press, 1971), chapters 1, 3, and 11.

United Nations, "Universal Declaration of Human Rights" (www.un.org/en/documents/udhr).

"What the World Eats," Time.com (www.time.com/time/photogallery/0,29307,1626519_1373664,00.html). Visual presentations of different families' diets and budgets.

Questions

1. Does "globalization" require global civics?

2. On what grounds is global civics necessary and feasible?

3. Concentrating on Africa, Asia, or South America as a case study, how plausible is it to establish a sense of global civics among the citizenry?

4. Consider Appiah's description of cultural "contamination." Does this constitute cosmopolitanism? Does it require global civics? How does it relate to justice?

5. Considering human progress so far, what has constrained global civics?

PART I: INTERCONNECTIONS

Week 2: The Environment

Ultimately, we are all connected through the environment. This includes the air, water, and ecological systems on which human life depends and that cannot be contained by international borders. Perhaps this fact is the main source of what has pulled-pushed humanity together, drawing each one of us to the other. The most salient common environmental problem facing the world today is human-generated climate change, the prospect that emissions of greenhouse gases are—like the panels of a greenhouse—warming the earth in ways that will lead to radical changes in the environment, including sea level rise, new weather patterns, and changes in ecosystems and the sustainability of agriculture. Since all human beings contribute to climate change, all human beings need to be part of the solution, and the international processes to respond to this problem have involved all of the world's countries. This does not mean, however, that each human being is equally responsible: residents of rich countries, especially large settler countries like the United States, Canada, and Australia, make a much greater contribution to climate change than residents of poor countries. The Kyoto Protocol, an international agreement on climate change, has finally come into force, with specific targets set for countries to reduce their emissions and a complex system of "carbon credits" that countries, companies, and producers can trade to allow high-emission countries to meet their targets. These carbon credits are themselves a resource for low-emitting poor countries, which can trade them to rich countries for badly needed capital. Already, a number of countries, rich and poor, have shown themselves capable of meeting their targets.

Readings and Other Media Sources

Climate Civics Institute (www.climatecivicsinstitute.org). A new institute devoted to sustainable practices to address climate change involving local communities and a global civic response to the problems of climate change.

Davis Guggenheim, director, *An Inconvenient Truth* (2006). A documentary about climate change.

Intergovernmental Panel on Climate Change (www.ipcc.ch). A vast resource of data and reports on climate change.

Peter Singer, "One Atmosphere," in *One World*, 2nd ed. (Yale University, 2004). A leading ethicist discusses climate change in simple language and proposes a simple way of allotting each human being's entitlement to carbon emission.

United Nations Framework Convention on Climate Change (http://unfccc.int/2860.php). Provides the text of the Kyoto Protocol and information on the operation of its associated mechanisms, including the emissions trading system and the Clean Development Mechanism.

Questions

1. Are the mechanisms to address international climate change fair?
2. Can international agreements concerning climate change be enforced?

Week 3: Resources

We all live on the same planet, and many religions and philosophies have taught that the earth belongs to the people of the world in common. And yet the use and control of resources has led to some of humanity's most severe and intractable conflicts. Thomas Pogge and Leif Wenar are two political philosophers who have examined our contemporary regime of resource rights and argue that we are all, as consumers, implicated in the conflicts and harms that unequal control over resources engenders. Both argue for particular reforms so that some of the worst results of this inequality can be avoided, and both suggest that considerable progress could be made simply by enforcing existing or previously existing conventions. The situation is further complicated by the problems of international environmental coordination discussed in week 2. Is it fair that poor countries should be kept from developing their resources to reduce their environmental impact? Are environmental problems in some countries necessary for the growth of all countries?

Readings

Extractive Industries Transparency Initiative (http://eiti.org). This initiative is an attempt to eliminate the worst results of the trade in resources, including conflicts, corruption, and inequality, through companies disclosing the price they pay for resources.

Global Witness, "Conflict Diamonds" (www.globalwitness.org/campaigns/onflict/conflict-diamonds). Global Witness is a nongovernmental organization devoted to addressing the negative effects of resource extraction. The page outlining its campaign regarding conflict diamonds contains a video critical of the Kimberley Process in practice.

Homi Kharas and Geoffrey Gertz, "The New Global Middle Class: A Cross-Over from West to East," paper, Wolfensohn Center for Development (Brookings, 2010).

Kimberley Process (www.kimberleyprocess.com/). The Kimberley Process is a scheme involving governments, industry, and civil society groups that allows member countries to certify their diamonds to consumers as "conflict free."

Thomas Pogge, "The Bounds of Nationalism," in *World Poverty and Human Rights* (Cambridge, U.K.: Polity, 2008), chapter 5. Pogge describes how the resources under the seabed were to be used for the benefit of the world's poor before this regime was altered by the world's wealthier countries.

Thomas Pogge, "A Global Resources Dividend" (www.hughlafollette.com/eip3/global.resources.dividend.pdf).

Leif Wenar, "Property Rights and the Resource Curse," April 30, 2007 (www.policyinnovations.org/ideas/innovations/data/resource_curse_1).

Edward Zwick, director, *Blood Diamond* (2006).

Questions

1. What is the resource curse?
2. Should the benefits of the globe's resources be shared *equally*?

3. Are individual consumers responsible for the plight of those harmed by conflicts over resources or those not benefiting by the extraction of resources from their communities? How does this relate to climate change and climate refugees?

Week 4: Trade and Capital

The force that most unites people across borders is, arguably, trade. In supermarkets consumers from wealthy countries can find products from poor countries that were picked only the day before. The production of green beans in Kenya for markets in London, for example, has been lauded as an important source of income for Kenya's poor farmers and farm laborers. Nevertheless, that example of trade is also criticized for entailing unsustainable food miles and inducing farmers to grow "cash crops" instead of food for the local community. Indeed, the entire structure of global trade has been targeted by activists, who see it as a system regulated to the advantage of wealthy countries and the large corporations based there. Similarly, the role of international capital and debt is held to prevent heavily indebted poor nations from being able to provide essential benefits to their populations, especially where International Monetary Fund and World Bank interventions have urged privatization of essential services, such as water and health care. The governance structures of the World Trade Organization, the World Bank, and the International Monetary Fund have been accused of effectively excluding poor nations.

One response to some of these concerns about trade and the power of large corporations has been a growing and largely uncoordinated switch by consumers to "fair trade" in certain products. Fair trade labeling is supposed to guarantee that the producer received a fair price for his product and, in a gesture toward democratic participation, that the products have been cooperatively produced. There also have been campaigns to certify certain cities and towns as "fair trade towns," indicating that the town government and a certain number of businesses use and promote fair trade goods.

Readings and Other Media Sources

Joel Bakan, writer; Mark Achbar and Jennifer Abbott, directors, *The Corporation* (2003). A documentary exploring the corporation's status as a legal person and its role in the global order; it features both prominent corporate insiders and critics of the corporation's role in international society. Available at www.youtube.com/view_play_list?p=FA50FBC214A6CE87.

Democracy Now, "An Hour with Vandana Shiva, Indian Scientist and Leading Critic of Corporate Globalization" (www.democracynow.org/2003/11/27/an_hour_with_vandana_shiva_indian). An interview with a leading critic of the World Trade Organization and "neoliberal globalization."

Fairtrade Labeling Organizations International (www.fairtrade.net). The largest coalition of fair trade certification organizations.

Fairtrade Towns (www.fairtradetowns.org). An international fair trade towns site.

Mark Francis and Nick Francis, directors, *Black Gold* (2006). A documentary juxtaposing the global North and South in the coffee trade.

Amrita Narlikar, "Fairness in International Trade Negotiations: Developing Countries in the GATT and WTO," *The World Economy* 29, no. 8 (2006): 1005–29.

Richard Peet, *Unholy Trinity: The IMF, World Bank and WTO,* 2nd ed. (London: Zed Books, 2009).

Joseph E. Stiglitz, Bert Koenders, and Jose Antonio Ocampo, "Reform of the International Monetary and Financial System," September 21, 2009 (www.cceia.org/resources/video/data/000265). A video on the contemporary problems of the international trade and monetary system; includes input from one of the International Monetary Fund's best-known critics, Joseph Stiglitz.

Questions

1. Should international financial institutions be democratized? Would this lead to imprudent decisions by some states?

2. Corporations are often conceived as persons, with analogous rights, including to intellectual property. Should they be understood as having rights similar to and sometimes against individual human beings?

3. To what degree are notions of justice and equity necessary within international trade institutions?

Week 5: The Global Public Sphere

The "global public sphere" is the global version of the domestic public sphere, the space where people meet in public to discuss matters of public interest. In the global case, the public sphere involves the spread of information about and critical discussion of issues concerning the environment, resources, and trade, among other things. Both global and domestic public spheres have been transformed through the spread and development of the Internet and, especially in the poorer parts of the world, through the spread of cheap cell phones. Before the spread of cell phones, it was difficult for farmers to learn the prices their crops would fetch in the larger towns; the only people who could tell them were the middlemen who were buying the crops from them. Now they have as much information as the people with whom they are bargaining. In many poor countries, cell phones and laptops are allowing doctors to remotely treat people in rural villages. Although Internet access is uneven across the global South, it is improving, and it is easier than ever for poorer and wealthier communities to work together. More important, it is difficult for authoritarian regimes to stop the flow of information across their borders or to prevent people from coordinating their activities to document human rights violations and mount more effective resistance. The Internet has also been harnessed in innovative ways to work on the problems of poverty and to promote corporate social responsibility. It also helps individuals to do their global civic duty more easily. The most obvious example of this is the spread of "carbon offsetting": initially, if you wanted to offset the carbon produced by air travel, for example, you had to visit a specialist website. Now the opportunity to offset is being offered as just another option by large travel websites like Orbitz.

Readings and Other Media Sources

Bill Baue, Marcy Murningham, and Jane Nelson, "Web 2.0 and Corporate Accountability," Carnegie Council on Ethics and International Affairs video, podcast, and transcript (www.cceia.org/resources/audio/data/000410).

Hunger Site (www.thehungersite.com/clickToGive/home.faces?siteId=1). The Hunger Site is an attempt to use Internet advertising techniques to bring food to hungry people. Among other features and causes, it includes a button that visitors can click so that the site's sponsors will donate food for free.

Zenobia Ismail and Paul Graham, "Citizens of the World? Africans, Media and Telecommunications," Afrobarometer Briefing Paper 69, May 2009 (www.afrobarometer.org/abbriefing.html).

Justmeans (www.justmeans.com). Justmeans is a "web 2.0" corporate social responsibility website that allows people from all over the world to participate in discussions, often involving senior executives of the firms involved, about corporations' global accountability, responsibility, and impact.

Kiva (www.kiva.org). Kiva is an innovative microfinance site, where individuals interested in making loans to people in poor countries are put in contact with people interested in taking out a microfinance loan.

Sharon LaFraniere, "Cellphones Catapult Rural Africa to 21st Century," *New York Times*, August 25, 2005 (www.nytimes.com/2005/08/25/international/africa/25africa.html).

Questions

1. Does the Internet free up people to act in altruistic ways, or does it reduce everything to a commodity?

2. Is the opportunity to comment on matters of global public interest the essence of global civics? Is it enough?

3. Does inequality in access to the Internet and mobile phone technology tend to replicate itself or decrease with use?

4. What opportunities, if any, do the new media and technologies present for a shared sense of global humanity?

Week 6: Global Civil Society

Although there are many different accounts of what constitutes civil society, it is usually held to refer to associations of people that are not part of the state, including everything from churches and unions to political and community organizations. As a result, it encompasses a wide variety of groups not all of which are benign or "civil," in the sense of respecting other members of society. Global civil society involves groups that are active in global affairs and with global concerns. Because these groups are, by definition, nongovernmental organizations (NGOs), the term has become identified with some of the largest NGOs active in the development, peace, and human rights fields, such as Oxfam, Médecins Sans Frontières, and Amnesty International. But this gives a misleading impression of both the potential and the operation of civil society groups concerned with international problems. As the example of polio eradication in Nigeria illustrates, coalitions formed to solve a particular problem can involve a very complex set of groups, from large philanthropic foundations to the local grassroots action committees of poor areas. The Nigerian initiative combined the efforts of the World Health Organization, UNICEF, and other international organizations with the support of the Bill and Melinda Gates Foundation and Rotary International (whose members across the world have given $1.5 billion as of 2010 and volunteer to immunize people across the world). In places like Kano State in Nigeria, where local resistance to vaccination led to an outbreak that spread polio to countries as far as Botswana, they teamed up with governmental organizations, religious leaders, and local civil society groups like the Kano State Polio Victims' Trust and local Rotary chapters.

A variety of civil society groups are given a formal role in some international institutions, such as the UN's Economic and Social Council. But these complex forms of participation do not mean that civil society groups are immune from criticism: the role of unelected NGOs in both international and domestic political spheres is cause for democratic concern, a concern that is compounded when big international NGOs engage with poor local communities. Thus while participants and supporters of civil society are being civic, in the general sense, it is a matter of contention whether they are helping or not. It has also been argued that civil society is being asked to do too much and that states are abdicating their responsibility in key areas. When NGOs are supplying basic services, such supply is vulnerable to fluctuations in the NGO's funding and sense of its own mission, and not subject to the direct democratic control that Amartya Sen identified as crucial to development as freedom.

Readings and Other Media Sources

Celia W. Dugger and Donald G. McNeil Jr., "Rumor, Fear and Fatigue Hinder Final Push to End Polio," *New York Times,* March 20, 2006 (www.nytimes.com/2006/03/20/international/asia/20polio.html; www.rotaryeclubny1.com/PolioOnBrink.htm).

Michael Edwards, "Civil Society," *The Encyclopedia of Informal Education,* 2005 (www.infed.org/association/civil_society.htm). A brief account of the role and problems of civil society.

Michael Edwards, *Just Another Emperor? The Myths and Realities of Philanthrocapitalism* (New York: Demos, 2008), downloadable for free from (www.futurepositive.org/emperor.php). A critique, by a leading theorist of civil society, of the new model of philanthropy associated with very wealthy individuals.

Global Polio Eradication Initiative (www.polioeradication.org). An initiative combining the efforts of the World Health Organization, UNICEF and other international organizations with the Bill and Melinda Gates Foundation and Rotary International.

Margaret E. Keck and Kathryn Sikkink, *Activists beyond Borders* (Cornell University Press, 1998). The classic account of transnational civil society networks.

Kenneth Newton, "Trust, Social Capital, Civil Society, and Democracy," *International Political Science Review* 22, no. 2 (2001): 201–14.

"Nigeria Deals with Polio Outbreak," *PBS Newshour,* video, April 14, 2009 (www.pbs.org/newshour/extra/video/blog/2009/04/nigeria_deals_with_polio_outbr.html).

Hildy Teegen, Jonathan P. Doh, and Sushil Vachani, "The Importance of Nongovernmental Organizations (NGOs) in Global Governance and Value Creation: An International Business Research Agenda," *Journal of International Business Studies* 35, no. 6 (2004): 463–83.

Mark E. Warren, "Can Participatory Democracy Produce Better Selves? Psychological Dimensions of Habermas's Discursive Model of Democracy," in "Political Theory and Political Psychology," special issue, *Political Psychology* 14, no. 2 (1993): 209–34.

Questions

1. Is civil society action democratic participation?

2. How should international civil society organizations cope with inequalities of wealth and power between the organizations and local communities?

3. Beyond mobilization on feminist, ecological, peace, and antinuclear issues, what other issues should social movements be concerned with?

4. How relevant is social and political trust in the ability of civil society to deliver on basic services?

Week 7: Religion

Religion is a form of association and solidarity that crosses boundaries—and not just physical ones. The world's major religions unite people from different classes, ethnic groups, linguistic communities, and heritages. Perhaps the most well-known case of conscious transborder identification is the Muslim *ummah*, or "community of believers." It is hard to say whether religion has been more of a force for peace or for conflict in human history. Concern about religious conflict and a sense of the importance of spirituality in global justice led the Parliament of the World's Religions, with the initiative of the important Swiss theologian Hans Küng, to promote a "global ethic," based on a set of values that can be affirmed by all religious traditions as well as by secular persons. Following the slogan "no rights without responsibilities," the Universal Declaration of Human Responsibilities consists mostly of a list of responsibilities and active attitudes that the declarers deem necessary to global justice and peace. Although its detractors claim that it avoids conflicts between religions rather than mediates them, the global ethic has attracted a lot of support from leaders around the world and has inspired people who believe that justice and human rights cannot be fully embraced without some spiritual basis and commitment.

Readings

Benedict Anderson, *Imagined Communities: Reflections on the Origin and Spread of Nationalism* (London: Verso, 1983).

Global Ethic Foundation (http://www.weltethos.org/dat-english/index. htm). Website contains the "Declaration toward a Global Ethic" and "A Universal Declaration of Human Responsibilities."

Hans Küng , "Global Ethic and Human Responsibilities" (www.scu.edu/ ethics/practicing/focusareas/global_ethics/laughlin-lectures/global-ethic-human-responsibility.html). A description of the development of the global ethic.

Hans Küng, *A Global Ethic for Global Politics and Economics* (Oxford University Press, 1998). Applies the global ethic to the problems of global politics and economics.

Hans Küng, ed., *Yes to a Global Ethic* (New York: Continuum, 1996). Contains responses by many world leaders to the global ethic.

Amin Maalouf, *In the Name of Identity: Violence and the Need to Belong* (New York: Arcade, 2001).

Organization of the Islamic Conference (http://www.oic-oci.org). The Islamic Conference is an international coalition of countries interested in the welfare of the *ummah*; the website covers its political activities and some of the conventions it has promoted, including the Cairo Declaration on Human Rights in Islam (www.oic-oci.org/english/article/ human.htm). The Cairo Declaration has been criticized for not including sufficient gender equality and religious freedom.

Mogobe Ramose, "The Philosophy of Ubuntu and Ubuntu as a Philosophy," in *The African Philosophy Reader,* edited by P. H. Coetzee and A. P. J. Raux, 2nd ed. (New York: Routledge, 2003), pp. 230–38.

Questions

1. Do human rights and democracy require a spiritual commitment to the equality and dignity of all human beings? If some religions prescribe different roles for men and women, is this compatible with the equal worth of all human beings?

2. Consider the list of responsibilities outlined in the declarations associated with the global ethic. Are these reasonable demands on the world's

people, regardless of their beliefs? Could or should a secular person endorse the global ethic?

3. Do ethical principles have a universal appeal? What opportunities do they present for a global civics?

PART II: RIGHTS AND RESPONSIBILITIES

Week 8: Civil Rights. I: The International Criminal Court and the Responsibility to Protect

The International Criminal Court (ICC) in the Hague, established by the Rome Statute in 1998, tries individuals accused of the most serious crimes against other people. It is the first general court of this type, replacing earlier tribunals designed to cover particular cases and conflicts. It can act against alleged criminals at the urging of the states that have agreed to the statute, the UN Security Council, or at the request of its own prosecutor. The genocides of the twentieth century, of which the emblematic example is the Holocaust, gave rise to both the desire for a tribunal to try those accused of "crimes against humanity" and the need for an international convention to enable intervention to prevent or end future genocides.

The 1948 Convention on the Prevention and Punishment of the Crime of Genocide (the Genocide Convention) permits just such humanitarian interventions. However, the important role of state sovereignty in the UN Charter has meant that the Genocide Convention has never triggered an intervention, even in the cases of Rwanda in 1994 or in the contested case of Darfur in the early twenty-first century. In response to the perceived weakness of the Genocide Convention, a new doctrine, the Responsibility to Protect (R2P), has been gaining acceptance in the international community. This doctrine maintains that states do not have sovereignty unconditionally but only insofar as they are able to protect their people from the worst crimes. If they cannot, then R2P licenses the international community to aid them in doing so, and if they still cannot, or if the state is responsible for the crimes, then the UN Security Council may authorize an intervention to protect that state's people. One of the most interesting aspects of R2P, as it is increasingly understood, is the suggestion that state sovereignty is related to popular sovereignty, namely, that if a state's actions show that it is grossly indifferent to the will of its people, then it is not entitled to the protections of a sovereign state from interference within its borders. It has been argued, however, that R2P has not been applied systematically; for example critics contrast the inaction in Rwanda to the response to some conflicts in Europe.

Readings and Other Media Sources

Mike DeWitt, director, *Worse than War* (2009); also available at www. pbs.org/wnet/worse-than-war/the-film/watch-worse-than-war/24. A documentary, based on the book of the same title by Daniel Goldhagen about genocide, featuring interviews with perpetrators and victims.

International Commission on Intervention and State Sovereignty, "The Responsibility to Protect," December 2001 (www.iciss.ca/report-en.asp).

International Criminal Court (www.icc-cpi.int). Contains the Rome Statute and individual cases.

Steven Kull, "Listening to the Voice of Humanity," *Kosmos*, Spring-Summer (2010): 26–29. (www.kosmosjournal.org/kjo2/backissue/s2010/index.shtml).

Office of the United Nations High Commissioner for Human Rights, "International Covenant on Civil and Political Rights" (www2.ohchr.org/english/law/ccpr.htm).

World Public Opinion.Org, "People in 17 of 21 Nations Say Governments Should Put International Law Ahead of National Interest," November 2, 2009 (www.worldpublicopinion.org/pipa/articles/btjustice human_rightsra/643.php?lb=bthr&pnt=643&nid=&id=).

Pamela Yates, director, "The Reckoning: The Battle for the International Criminal Court" (2009; http://vimeo.com/9160246). A documentary about the workings and disputes surrounding the ICC and its prosecutor Luis Moreno Ocampo.

Questions

1. Critics of the International Criminal Court and the Responsibility to Protect argue that they will be used to intervene in the affairs of states that are not guilty of committing or failing to prevent the most serious

crimes, on the basis of an international politics that favors the more pow-erful states. Do you think that these dangers make the ICC and R2P fundamentally flawed?

2. Does state sovereignty necessarily depend on the will of the people? Does the relationship between the two need to be enhanced?

Week 9: Civil and Legal Rights. II: Refugees

One of the more effectively protected human rights is the right to seek asylum, or refugee status, when, in the words of the 1967 version of the United Nations Convention on the Status of Refugees,

> a person who owing to well-founded fear of being persecuted for reasons of race, religion, nationality, membership of a particu-lar social group or political opinion, is outside the country of his nationality and is unable or, owing to such fear, is unwilling to avail himself of the protection of that country; or who, not having a nationality and being outside the country of his former habitual residence as a result of such events, is unable or, owing to such fear, is unwilling to return to it.

In such cases a person can claim refugee status and has the right to have his or her case for asylum considered according to certain legal principles, including due process standards equivalent to those of citizens of the country in question. This is a legal right that all human beings have and one which transcends borders. Unfortunately, it is a right that many people need. According to the Office of the UN High Commissioner for Refugees, there were 43.3 million "forcibly displaced persons" world-wide in December 2009, about 27.1 million of whom were "internally displaced persons," that is, individuals forcibly displaced to another part of the country they usually live in. There were at least 6.6 million "state-less persons," people who cannot successfully make a claim to citizenship in a particular state. These statistics do not include people forced to move by economic necessity or by natural factors such as climate change.

As travel has become easier, there have been increasing numbers of people who avail themselves of this right, in some cases because economic migration is prohibited. Because countries are faced with unequal numbers of people asking for refugee status, different proposals for sharing the burdens of asylum have emerged. Thus a right that transcends borders and involves movement across borders has led to new levels of international cooperation, including efforts like those of the United Kingdom's Gateway Protection Program and the United States' Resettlement and Placement Program, which transport and resettle people who live in refugee camps to wealthy countries. It has also led to considerable repression as countries attempt to keep out people who might make claims to asylum.

Readings and Other Media Sources

Guy S. Goodwin-Gill, "Refugees: Challenges to Protection," *International Migration Review* 35, no. 1 (2001): 130–42. An assessment of the history and prospects of refugee protection by the world's leading scholar of refugee law.

Megan Mylan and Jon Shenk, directors, *Lost Boys of Sudan* (2004). A documentary that follows Sudanese refugees across Africa, from Sudan to the United States.

Nashville Public Television, "Next Door Neighbors: Somali" (2008, www.youtube.com/watch?v=Qlo200gHkQ8). A public television program about Somali refugees resettled in Nashville, Tennessee.

United Nations High Commissioner for Refugees (www.unhcr.org). Contains the text of the 1951 United Nations Convention Relating to the Status of Refugees, statistics about displaced persons, and more, including "2009 Global Trends: Refugees, Asylum-Seekers, Returnees, Internally Displaced and Stateless Persons" (www.unhcr.org/4c11f0be9.html).

United Nations High Commissioner for Refugees, "International Solidarity and Burden-Sharing in All Its Aspects: National, Regional and International Responsibilities for Refugees," September 1998 (www.unhcr.org/cgi-bin/texis/vtx/refworld/rwmain?page=search&docid=4a54bc2f0&skip=0&query=burden%20sharing).

Michael Winterbottom, director, *In this World* (2003). A fictional film about two Afghan refugees' journey to London and the obstacles they experience.

Questions

1. How would you describe the relationship between national democratic citizenship and the right to exclude others?

2. Only individuals with "a well-founded fear of persecution" are entitled to asylum. Can we ethically make a distinction between them and people fleeing poverty and the destruction of their homes through climate change?

3. Does "burden sharing" among states and within regions promote justice for refugees and other migrants?

Week 10: Political Rights. I: The United Nations

As the earlier discussion of intervention (week 8) suggests, most individuals find their greatest opportunities to assert their political rights in the states of which they are citizens. But through those states they can participate in the United Nations, which was formed after World War II, in the words of its charter's Preamble, by the "peoples" of the world

> to save succeeding generations from the scourge of war, which twice in our lifetime has brought untold sorrow to mankind, and to reaffirm faith in fundamental human rights, in the dignity and worth of the human person, in the equal rights of men and women and of nations large and small, and to establish conditions under which justice and respect for the obligations arising from treaties and other sources of international law can be maintained, and to promote social progress and better standards of life in larger freedom. . . .

The UN, and its component organizations have been working on the goals of peace, human rights, and development ever since, but the process has been characterized by political conflicts among the five permanent members of its Security Council and between these permanent members and coalitions of other countries in the General Assembly. People, and peoples, appear at the UN as states, and the UN's charter reinforces the primacy of sovereignty, as noted in a previous discussion. Accordingly, individual human beings cannot assert their political rights at the global level. To this end, various reforms have been proposed to permit a more democratic world. We examine one of them: David Held's vision for overlapping levels of democratic government. One of the main criticisms of the UN has been the presence of authoritarian regimes and violators of human rights in the UN's representative bodies and even its human rights institutions. It has often been suggested that a representative assembly of democratic states would deny legitimacy to states that violate the rights of their people and encourage them to adopt effective democratic institutions. Such an international organization already exists: the Community of Democracies.

Readings

Michael Bratton and Robert Mattes, "Neither Consolidating nor Fully Democratic: The Evolution of African Political Regimes, 1999–2008," Afrobarometer Briefing Paper 67, May 2009 (www.afrobarometer. org/papers/AfrobriefNo67_19may09_final.pdf).

Community of Democracies (www.community-democracies.org/). The Community of Democracies is a coalition of democratic countries dedicated to the promotion of "democratic norms and institutions." It was founded in 2000 by delegations from over 100 countries.

E. Gyimah-Boadi and Daniel Armah Attoh, "Are Democratic Citizens Emerging in Africa? Evidence from the Afrobarometer," Afrobarometer Briefing Paper 70, May 2009 (www.afrobarometer.org/papers/ AfrobriefNo70_21may09.pdf).

David Held, "Democracy: From City-States to a Cosmopolitan Order?" *Political Studies* 40, supplement s1 (1992): 10–39. Held proposes complex structures for cosmopolitan democracy, involving overlapping local, regional, and global representative bodies, including an assembly of democratic states. He also gives a good overview of the historical development of different conceptions of democracy and citizenship.

United Nations, "Charter of the United Nations" (www.un.org/en/ documents/charter/index.shtml).

United Nations, "Reform at the United Nations" (www.un.org/reform). The UN's own view of reform. Includes access to the important 2005 reform document, "In Larger Freedom," which includes a greater emphasis on the Responsibility to Protect.

Questions

1. How should the Security Council be reformed, if at all?

2. Can one draw any particular link between national democracy and global democracy?

3. Is democracy possible at the global level? Are Held's proposals realizable in practice?

4. How should we interpret the emergence of other global institutions (such as the Group of Seventy-Seven, Group of Twenty, and others)?

Week 11: Political Rights. II: Continental and Regional Bodies

David Held's discussion of cosmopolitan or global democracy places a considerable emphasis on regional organizations, such as the European Union (EU) and the African Union (AU). The EU, in particular, has attracted a lot of attention from advocates of global democracy because it has a complex set of institutions, including an executive European Commission, a European Council of the member states, and a directly elected European Parliament. It also has courts to adjudicate disputes between members. Because its member states are also members of the Council of Europe, European citizens enjoy the world's most substantial human rights protections through the European Court of Human Rights, where individuals can bring cases against governments that they think have violated their rights. The cornerstones of European integration are the four freedoms: the free movement of goods, capital, services, and people. These freedoms constitute part, but not all, of citizenship of the EU and have enabled remarkable transborder interconnections among citizens of the EU through trade and migration. That European citizenship is not just the opportunity to trade is what separates regional associations of states from free trade agreements like the North American Free Trade Agreement (NAFTA) or the *Mercado Común del Sur* (MERCOSUR). Regional associations are interested in promoting trade but also work together on solving problems and resolving conflicts that span borders. Elsewhere in the world, there are regional bodies and human rights systems that could someday permit similar solidarity across borders, with all the economic and security benefits that provides. Already, we see the AU, the Organization of American States, and the Association of Southeast Asian Nations taking on greater roles in securing peace and promoting trade.

Readings

African Union (www.africa-union.org). Website of the AU (formerly the Organization of African Unity), which includes the "Constitutive Act of the African Union," discussions of AU-backed interventions, and proposals for the greater integration of its member states.

Association of Southeast Asian Nations (www.asean.org). Website of the Association of Southeast Asian Nations, including material on its attempts at peacebuilding and promoting regional development, and on the Intergovernmental Commission on Human Rights.

Ulrich Beck, "Re-inventing Europe: A Cosmopolitan Vision," talk given at the Centre de Cultura Contemporània de Barcelona, October 27, 2005 (www.publicspace.org/en/text-library/eng/b004-re-inventing-europe-a-cosmopolitan-vision). The distinguished sociologist Ulrich Beck provides his own vision of a cosmopolitan Europe, which he controversially dubs an "empire of law and consensus," but one based on diversity and openness to foreigners.

European Union (http://europa.eu). The website of the EU, including opportunities to participate in discussions about EU policies.

Jürgen Habermas, "Toward a Cosmopolitan Europe," *Journal of Democracy* 14, no. 4 (2003): 86–100. The great German philosopher Habermas describes what citizenship and institutions would be necessary for Europe to be truly cosmopolitan and democratic.

Organization of American States (www.oas.org/en/default.asp). Website of the Organization of American States, including videos about its members' "common values" and its role in election monitoring in the region.

Questions

1. Both Habermas and Beck argue that global interdependence means that the sovereign nation-state can no longer serve as the basis for democratic self-determination. Are regional unions the answer to this problem?

Or do they lack the solidarity necessary for people to identify with them as the main source of legitimate law?

2. Can regional unions be seen as useful in promoting global justice?

3. Beck argues that states can no longer effectively exclude would-be migrants, often cultural "others," from their territories. Does this encourage regional solutions or does it only encourage exclusion—"Fortress Europe"—on a larger scale?

Week 12: Social Rights. I: Human Security and the Voices of the Poor

To assert their legal and political rights, human beings also need their economic and social rights met. Although many people now enjoy access to clean water, adequate nutrition, shelter, health care, and education that did not do so previously, billions of human beings still lack access to safe drinking water, appropriate nutrients and basic and inexpensive medical treatments, such as rehydration salts. The International Covenant on Economic, Social, and Cultural Rights has been ratified by 160 countries. A number of critics claim that people cannot have a right to these things the way they have civil and political rights, either because they require too much of states or because it is unclear who has a duty to provide these things for people who lack them. But considerable progress has been made in understanding how these rights might be implemented and how it can be clearly determined who is obligated to do what and when. Originating in the work of philosopher Henry Shue, the notion that everyone has obligations to first "respect," then "protect," and then "fulfill" these rights has become the canonical understanding of how we should recognize our relationship to people who do not enjoy these rights, wherever they are.

As the role of protection in the list of obligations suggests, this rights-based understanding of basic needs can be understood another way, in terms of security. The idea of "human security" arose both from an awareness that there was more to security than simply protecting people from violence and from the way that poor people around the world talked about their condition. A focus on human security allows us to see how threatening it is to lack access to basic goods and also to better evaluate particular state policies. A state that spends a lot more on its military than it does on health care, for example, can be seen to be failing to provide human security to its population, however secure the populace is from physical assault.

Readings

Commission on Human Security (www.humansecurity-chs.org/index.html). Initiated by the government of Japan, the commission made its final report to the UN in 2003.

Asbjorn Eide, "Economic, Social and Cultural Rights as Human Rights," in *Economic, Social and Cultural Rights: A Textbook*, 2nd ed. (Leiden: Martinus Nijhoff Publishers, 2000), chapter 2 (www.wcl.american.edu/humright/hracademy/documents/EideClass1-Economicandsocialrightsashumanrights-AsbjornEide.pdf?rd=1). In this selection, Eide provides an account of the development of human economic, social, and cultural rights and how these rights impose obligations on states, substate actors, and individuals.

Office of the UN High Commissioner for Human Rights, "International Covenant on Economic, Social and Cultural Rights" (www2.ohchr.org/english/law/cescr.htm).

UN Development Program, *Human Development Report 1994: New Dimensions of Human Security* (http://hdr.undp.org/en/reports/global/hdr1994). This document initiated the discussion on human security.

World Bank, "Voices of the Poor" (http://go.worldbank.org/H1N8746X10). This webpage contains material from a remarkable study conducted by the World Bank, involving interviews with over 60,000 poor people from 60 countries, so that the concerns and attitudes of the world's poor could be heard in their own voices. This site allows access to the three books that resulted, an audio recording of some of the voices, and a description of how the interviews were conducted.

Questions

1. What emerges from your listening to the voices of the "poor"? Do you believe that "poor" people the world over want the same things, or do

differences in cultural and religious values mean that they are not talking about the same things?

2. Are economic and social rights human rights?

3. Are there adequate institutions (internationally) to sufficiently promote economic and social rights?

Week 13: Social Rights. II: Development as Freedom

The great Indian economist and philosopher Amartya Sen made a famous discovery about famine: famines do not occur under democratic regimes. That is why he titled his book *Development as Freedom,* because when people are able to influence their government through elections and freedom of the press and association, governments provide the services and supports necessary to prevent famine deaths in the case of sudden shocks to the food supply, whether through scarcity or a sharp rise in prices. Sen noted that far from being absolutely scarce during most famines, food is often exported from the famine-stricken country, and he noted that although India experienced famine in Bengal as recently as 1943, famines have not occurred—with the possible exception of Bihar in 1966—since India became an independent, democratic state. This observation shows the importance of poor people's agitation for important economic and social rights, and their need for the civil and political freedom to do so. The poor Indian state of Kerala is often cited as an example of the importance of democratic development. Despite its poverty it has achieved impressive results on literacy, health, and other development indicators. The "Kerala model" also has its critics, though, who suggest that these results are more apparent than real and disguise a downside of unemployment and economic stagnation.

Sen's observation also highlights the importance of international campaigns of solidarity. Both the South African Treatment Action Campaign and the international network Slum Dwellers International have used international pressure to achieve results in particular countries. In the case of Slum Dwellers International, the network is truly transnational, involving homeless, displaced, and poorly accommodated people from across the world in a democratic, transnational network.

Readings

"Interview with Sheela Patel of Slum Dwellers International" (http://vimeo.
com/6858544). In this video Sheela Patel, the founder-director of the
Society for Promotion of Area Resource Centers in Mumbai, discusses
the Slum Dwellers International model of democratic organization.

Amartya Sen, "The Importance of Democracy," in *Development as Freedom* (Oxford University Press, 1999), chapter 6.

Shack/Slum Dwellers International (www.sdinet.org). Website contains
campaigns, educational curricula, and bottom-up strategies for enu-
merating slum dwellers for political action, from underhoused communities across the global South, from Brazil to Africa to India.

Treatment Action Campaign (www.tac.org.za/community). Includes
campaigns with an international focus and concern for issues beyond
treatment for HIV/AIDS. Using international and national solidarity,
the campaign successfully forced the South African government to
provide some treatment for HIV under its constitutional provisions for
the right to health.

René Véron, "The 'New' Kerala Model: Lessons for Sustainable Development," *World Development* 29, no. 4 (2001): 601–17. This article
describes the fortunes of the "Kerala model," paying particular attention to the role of decentralized democracy and grassroots action.

Questions

1. Is grassroots democracy inefficient as a way to honor individuals'
social and economic rights?

2. How democratic is the use of international pressure by movements for
social and economic rights within a particular state?

Class Exercise in Preparation for Week 14

The class must split into four groups. Each pair of groups will be given a
topic that they will debate using opposing arguments:

—Groups 1 and 2: Global civics is an unattainable ideal.

—Groups 3 and 4: The world's youth have a considerable role to play
in the achievement of a global civics.

Each group will have fifteen minutes to make its case, with twenty minutes for discussion after each debate.

Week 14: Conclusion

In this final week, we consider the global interconnections and responsibilities that we have discussed so far and discuss the future of global civics. We will explore the prospects for cooperation across borders, and discuss whether there are trends or pressures toward more global political engagement and whether this will or could be accompanied by individual global civic action. Much of this discussion will examine recent events and the real prospects for global civic action for the individual members of the class, situated, as we all are, in their different and cross-cutting identities and communities. (If part of the course evaluation includes "action projects"—individual studies or efforts at global civic action—this would be a good time to present them.) Students might reflect on their participation in the deliberations of the course itself—does their participation reflect or model global civics?

We will review the theories of justice of John Rawls and Amartya Sen. In particular, we will use Rawls's idea of a "veil of ignorance" to consider the possibility of an ideal and hypothetical social contract. We will also consider the opposing approach of Amartya Sen, who focuses on achieving comparatively more just arrangements without reference to what he calls a "transcendental" conception of justice.

Readings

John Rawls, *A Theory of Justice* (Harvard University Press, 1999), chapters 1, 3, and 11.

Amartya Sen, *The Idea of Justice* (Harvard University Press, 2009), introduction and chapter 17.

UN Development Program, *Human Development Report 2002: Deepening Democracy in a Fragmented World* (http://hdr.undp.org/en/reports/global/hdr2002/chapters/). An important report on how the world could be made more democratic.

Questions

1. Are the democratic commitments put forth in the 2002 Human Development Report compromised by its focus on development?

2. What institutions are needed for global civics? Do these necessarily involve coercive power?

3. What responsibilities, if any, do we have to our fellow human beings?

Thought Experiments

Write an essay, in the context of global civics, advising the seven-billionth person, who will soon be born. What would you say to him or her?

or

Imagine a group of people attempting to agree to a global social contract under the conditions of Rawls's "veil of ignorance," in which they are unaware of their gender, wealth, religious or moral commitments, or any other aspect of their identities that distinguishes them from other people. What rights and responsibilities, institutions, and laws would these people agree to and why?

Notes

1. T. H. Marshall and Tom Bottomore, *Citizenship and Social Class* (London: Pluto Press, 1987). Selections available at http://academic.udayton.edu/clarakim/inequality/articles/1-intro/Marshall--Citizenship%20and%20Social%20Class.pdf.

Contributors

Hakan Altinay
Senior fellow at the Brookings Institution and former Yale World Fellow. Altinay lectures on global civics at various universities around the world.

Balveer Arora
Professor of political science and former rector of Jawaharlal Nehru University in New Delhi.

Murat Belge
Professor of comparative literature at Bilgi University in Istanbul.

Nabil Fahmy
Founding dean of the School of Global Affairs and Public Policy at the American University in Cairo.

Jonathan Fanton
Past president of the John D. and Catherine T. MacArthur Foundation, Chicago, and of the New School for Social Research in New York City. Fanton is also former chairman of the Board of Human Rights Watch.

Graham Finlay
Lecturer at the School of Politics and International Relations, University College Dublin.

Vusi Gumede
Associate professor of development studies at the University of Johannesburg and a former Yale World Fellow.

David Held
Professor of political science and codirector of the Center for the Study of Global Governance at the London School of Economics.

Tara Hopkins
Founding director of the Civic Involvement Program at Sabanci University in Istanbul.

Andrey Kortunov
President of the New Eurasia Foundation in Moscow and former president of the Moscow Public Science Foundation.

Ivan Krastev
Chairman of the Center for Liberal Strategies in Sofia.

Ricardo Lagos
Past president of Chile and former president of the Club of Madrid. Lagos served as the United Nations special envoy on climate change and currently teaches at Brown University as professor-at-large.

Trevor Manuel
Minister in charge of national planning for South Africa. He has also served as minister of finance and of trade and industry.

Edgar Pieterse
Professor and director of the African Centre for Cities at the University of Cape Town.

Thomas Pogge
Professor of philosophy and the director of the Global Justice Program at Yale University. Pogge also teaches at University of Oslo and the Australian National University.

Dani Rodrik
Professor of international political economy at the Kennedy School, Harvard University.

Dingli Shen
Professor of international relations and executive dean of the Institute of International Affairs at Fudan University in Shanghai.

Javier Solana
Past minister of foreign affairs of Spain, as well as former secretary general of NATO and high representative for Common Foreign and Security Policy of the European Union. Once a professor of physics, Solana now teaches global politics and economics at ESADE in Madrid.

Tosun Terzioğlu
Professor of mathematics and founding president of Sabanci University in Istanbul. Terzioğlu is the former president of the Scientific and Technological Research Council of Turkey.

Index

Gourevitch, Philip, 92
Grassroots movements, 56, 58–59
Great Experiment, The (Talbott), 94
Group of Eight countries (G-8; Canada,
	Russia, France, Germany, Italy, Japan,
	UK, U.S.), 38
Group of Seven countries (G-7; Canada,
	France, Germany, Italy, Japan, UK,
	U.S.), 14, 73
Group of Seventy-Seven countries
	(G-77; UN coalition of developing
	countries), 58
Group of Twenty countries (G-20; 19
	countries, EU), 34, 38, 58, 73, 74
Growth Commission for Africa, 62

Hansen, James, 91
Harvard University (U.S.), 44
Hawking, Steven, 91
Held, David, 28–31, 73, 74–75, 126, 127
Hobsbawm, Eric, 79
Holocaust, 92, 121
Human rights. *See* Rights; Universal Decla-
	ration of Human Rights
Human security, 129–30
Hunt, Lynn, 35

ICANN. *See* Internet Corporation for
	Assigned Names and Numbers
ICC. *See* International Criminal Court
IMF. *See* International Monetary Fund
Immigration and migration, 12
India: famine in, 131; global civics and
	Indian universities, 24–25; membership
	on the UN Security Council, 25, 58; as
	a moral leader, 36; societal responses
	in, 37; support for international laws
	in, 15
Intellectual property, 41
Interdependence. *See* Global
	interdependence
International Action Network on Small
	Arms, 93
International Campaign to Ban Landmines,
	93
International Commission on Education for
	Sustainable Development Practice, 27
International Covenant on Economic,
	Social, and Cultural Rights, 129

International Criminal Court (ICC), 11,
	27, 53, 79–80, 92, 121–22
International Labor Organization, 55
International laws, 14–15
International Monetary Fund (IMF), ix,
	73–74, 79, 113
International norms, 55
International Panel on Climate Change
	(IPCC), 91
International/supranational organizations,
	79
Internet: as a debate forum, 35; Fifth
	Power program and, 39; global and
	domestic public spheres and, 115;
	globalization of, 1; number of users,
	81; online communication and inter-
	action, 45; Russia and, 32; virtual citi-
	zens and, 50
Internet—websites: 350.org, 92; cait.wri.
	org (Climate Analysis Indicators Tool),
	91–92; dndi.org (Drugs for Neglected
	Diseases Initiative), 93; gapminder.org
	(Gapminder), 90; gci.org.uk
	(Contraction and Convergence), 92;
	globalgovernancewatch.org (Global
	Governance Watch), 94; globalzero.org
	(Global Zero), 93; iansa.org (Interna-
	tional Action Network on Small Arms),
	93; icbl.org (International Campaign to
	Ban Landmines), 93; ipcc.ch (Interna-
	tional Panel on Climate Change), 91;
	worldpublicopinion.org (World Public
	Opinion), 90; worldvaluessurvey.org
	(World Values Survey), 90. *See also
	end-of-chapter entries, "Readings"
	and "Readings and Other Media
	Sources"*
Internet Corporation for Assigned Names
	and Numbers (ICANN), 1, 55
IPCC. *See* International Panel on Climate
	Change
Ishiguro, Kazuo, 93

Jameson, Fredric, 104
Jawaharlal Nehru University (India),
	24–25
Jayadev, Arjun, 74
John D. and Catherine T. MacArthur
	Foundation (Chicago), 27
Justice, 7